# Present -ing K!

# Present -ing K!

**Jaeyoung Park**

**All The Korea
You May Not See**

# 0.

# A Journey Beyond Guides: Unveiling the Untold Korea

Hey there! If you're reading this, chances are you're planning a trip to South Korea, and that's absolutely awesome! Whether you already have a specific itinerary in mind or you're simply dreaming of visiting someday, let me assure you that you're in for a real treat. South Korea offers a wealth of opportunities for exploration, whether it's a short-term visit like a business trip or vacation, or a long-term stay for studying or working. Maybe you're a K-Pop or Korean drama enthusiast, eager to delve deeper into the country's vibrant culture. Regardless of your motivations, I'm confident that reading this book will enrich your knowledge about Korea, ignite your passion to visit, and enhance your overall experience.

Believe it or not, this is the first book written by a bona fide, full-blooded Korean native, exclusively for you fine foreign readers. Now, I don't mean to devalue those other guidebooks in English or other languages, but all of them were written by folks who barely scratched the surface of Korea on a quick visit. This book, though? It's the real deal, straight from the source.

As a Korean native, who's spent over five decades in Korea, I've acquired an exceptional understanding of the Korean language, culture, and history. From my school days all the way to graduate school, I've dove deep into a wide range of subjects, relished the diverse flavors of Korean cuisine, and explored numerous iconic landmarks across Korea. Yet, I'm fully aware that many Koreans have had similar experiences. So, what sets me apart as the author of this book, and what makes me the one behind this book? Allow me to share a few reasons that compelled me to undertake this endeavor.

One of the primary reasons is my background as a journalist. With over 20 years of experience in the healthcare media industry, my expertise lies in translating intricate medical concepts into easily understandable language for a broad audience. It's worth noting that I am also a doctor, although my current focus does not involve direct patient care. Throughout my career, I have published numerous articles, columns, and books on healthcare-related topics. Additionally, I have even authored a novel set in a hospital, which was later adapted into a popular TV drama. Writing is truly my forte, and I am confident in my ability to effectively convey the essence of Korea to readers.

Next, I'm a seasoned traveler with a true knack for planning and preparing for trips. My previous book, *The Art of Preparing for a Trip*, a humorous and unique collection of travel essays unfortunately not yet available in English, is a testament to my passion for traveling and planning. Some of my friends have even playfully referred to me as the "Bill Bryson of South Korea," so you could say that I'm a bit of a travel writer myself.

Furthermore, I have a profound passion for delectable cuisine and take great pleasure in exploring renowned restaurants and experimenting with various dishes in my own kitchen. While it may have been written some time ago, I also possess experience in writing about food and cooking. Undoubtedly, one of the most remarkable aspects of immersing oneself in Korea is the chance to savor its incredibly diverse and relatively undiscovered food culture. With that in mind, this book encompasses a multitude of captivating anecdotes and insights into the world of Korean cuisine.

Moreover, my globetrotting adventures have taken me to over 20 countries, and I even resided in the United States for a couple of years. Through these experiences, I've gained a unique perspective on how Korea stands apart from other nations and what aspects of Korean culture tend to captivate foreigners. I've discovered that outsiders often find fascination in things that locals may overlook or take for granted. Drawing from this understanding, I've crafted this book with a keen awareness of what foreign visitors find alluring about Korea. My goal is to provide readers with an informative and entertaining journey that showcases the intriguing aspects of Korean culture.

Last but certainly not least, the most crucial factor driving me to write this book is that no other Korean has ever embarked on a project quite like this. It's a thrilling and fulfilling endeavor to undertake something that has never been done before and to create a singular work that hasn't existed in the world until now, regardless of its perceived significance. This unwavering motivation has played a pivotal role in propelling me forward to pen this comprehensive book on Korea. I am genuinely excited to share my distinctive perspective with readers and offer a fresh take on the wonders of Korea that has yet to be explored.

Now, let me shoot straight with you. I won't claim that Korea is the absolute best country in the world - few would make such a bold assertion about South Korea as a top-tier travel destination. However, what I can assure you is that Korea is an incredibly enjoyable country, a place where you can create an abundance of unforgettable memories unlike anywhere else. It's a thrill to venture into Korea with little prior knowledge, and it's even more exciting to dive into the pages of *Lonely Planet Korea* before your trip. But mark my words, after reading this book, your journey to Korea will become infinitely more exhilarating.

There's a well-known phrase that every Korean is familiar with: "You can see as much as you know." And that's exactly what I'm here to do - help you see more, have a blast, and create countless memories in Korea by sharing an array of captivating stories. That's right, this book is all about stories, not just a repository of information. It's not your typical guidebook overflowing with details. There are already plenty of those on the market. If you haven't yet solidified your plans to visit Korea, this book will serve as an excellent starting point. However, if you're already in search of a plane ticket, it might be wise to also grab a conventional guidebook to supplement your journey.

Nevertheless, my genuine wish is for you to have the chance to experience this captivating country at least once. May you immerse yourself in the abundant wonders that you can hardly have in any other countries and create cherished memories that will last a lifetime. Until that day comes, I eagerly await your arrival in Korea, ready to share the enchantments and delights that await you. Safe travels, and see you soon!

Jaeyoung Park

**Contents**

# 1.

If you're only eating one meal, choose "samgyeopsal"

_____

Samgyeopsal. Now that's a tongue twister you'll want to master if you're planning a trip to Korea. Trust me, if there's only one meal you can savor during your time in Korea, let it be samgyeopsal. Samgyeopsal literally translates to "three-layered meat," referring to the pork belly, and it's a must-try dish. But, don't worry if pork isn't your thing or if you're following a vegetarian diet. Korea has an abundance of other delicious dishes for you to explore.

It's ridiculously easy to make — so easy, in fact, that it hardly even qualifies as a recipe. All you need to do is choose how you want to cut the meat - how thick, at what angle - and then throw it on the grill, sans seasoning. That's it, folks. But despite its straightforward preparation, there's something undeniably special about this dish. Sure, the quality of the meat is crucial, but so too are the ingredients that accompany it, and the myriad ways you can enjoy it.

Let's talk about how much Koreans adore pork belly. With a population of roughly 50 million people and around 10 million pigs in the country, that means there's practically one pig per family of five. While this may sound like a substantial number, the issue is that each pig only provides 15 kilograms of pork belly, meaning that South Korea needs to import this cut of meat from roughly a dozen other nations. There's even a running joke that Koreans have managed to devour all the pork belly in the world. Thankfully, not many countries share the same pork belly obsession, allowing Korea to import it at a reasonable price.

There is a reason for everything, including why pork belly is a beloved dish in Korea and not as popular in other countries. Pork belly is rich in fat, which can make it too greasy for certain palates when consumed on its own. In the Western world, it is often cured and turned into bacon. However, in Korea, pork belly is elevated to new heights by pairing it with an array of complementary ingredients. It's commonly served alongside the spicy kick of kimchi, fresh vegetables like mushrooms, onions, lettuce, perilla leaf (known as "kkaennip"), garlic, bean sprouts ("kongnamul"), and scallions. And let's not forget the delectable "ssamjang" sauce, made with the flavorful "doenjang". Other seasonings like salt, pepper, and sesame oil add the perfect finishing touch.

It's understandable if you're feeling a tad bewildered. There's already a bunch of unfamiliar words swirling around. But fret not, my friend. We'll dive into all the nitty-gritty details later. For now, let's keep the momentum going and forge ahead.

No need to mix everything up at once. Depending on the restaurant, you may get a different selection of ingredients. Koreans enjoy pork belly by savoring each bite with different accompaniments like kimchi, lettuce, perilla leaf, and so on. In fact, Koreans have countless variations of the one dish they call pork belly, with each place offering its unique twist.

Now, let's skip the lengthy explanations and dive right into the experience of going to a samgyeopsal restaurant. As this dish holds a special place in Korean cuisine, numerous restaurants across the country serve it. In bustling cities like Seoul, you need only walk a few minutes in any direction to come across a pork belly restaurant. However, don't expect to see an English sign that says "samgyeopsal" outside these establishments. While the Korean term for pork belly (samgyeopsal) may be visible somewhere on the exterior of the restaurant, it may not be discernible to someone who can't read Korean (like you). Koreans just have a sixth sense when it comes to spotting samgyeopsal joints.

Luckily, a multitude of restaurants proudly showcase mouthwatering images of pork belly on their exteriors. So, if your eyes feast upon a tantalizing picture featuring layers of succulent fat and juicy meat, congratulations, you've stumbled upon a samgyeopsal haven. And if the irresistible aroma of sizzling meat dances its way to your nostrils, accompanied by the sight of smokestacks elegantly poised above each table, rest assured, my friend, you've hit the pork belly jackpot.

In the vast sea of samgyeopsal restaurants, there are those that flourish and those that struggle to make their mark. In fact, there are even establishments so wildly popular that you might find yourself patiently queuing for over an hour, eagerly anticipating your turn to dive into samgyeopsal's flavorsome gratification. (Fear not, for I shall provide a separate list of these highly coveted gems within the pages of this book.) However, rest assured that as long as you steer clear of desolate, empty establishments devoid of patrons, you can confidently step into any restaurant without a worry. Finding a place where you can indulge in the distinct and savory pleasure of pork belly should be a breeze.

As you enter a samgyeopsal restaurant, prepare yourself for a few delightful surprises. Right away, your attention will be drawn to a gas stove positioned at the center of your table. It could be a convenient portable burner like those used for camping, or a purpose-built fire pit seamlessly integrated into the tabletop. If you spot an intriguing hole in the middle of the table, you've chosen a great restaurant. Before you know it, a captivating spectacle will unfold as the charcoal fire roars to life, a clear sign of a more upscale and sophisticated establishment.

As you acquaint yourself with the idiosyncrasies of the table, a friendly server will approach you to take your order, and it's quite common for them not to provide you with a physical menu. Instead, you'll likely find menus adorning the walls, as Koreans are renowned for their efficiency and swift service. But worry not, my friend. Simply utter the magical word "samgyeopsal" and hold up the appropriate number of fingers to indicate the size of your group. Don't hesitate to request a taste of "soju", a beloved Korean alcoholic beverage that comes highly recommended. Of course, if you prefer, you can also opt for a refreshing beer. But since you're in Korea, it's worth embracing the opportunity to try their favorite libation and immerse yourself in the local culture.

If you find yourself lucky, or if the waiter is quick to catch on, then you can proceed smoothly from there. However, in the event that the waiter strictly adheres to the field manual and doesn't have a strong command of English, the conversation may pose a bit more of a challenge.

The likely inquiry from the waiter will be, "What kind of soju?" or "What kind of beer?" There are a variety of brands of soju and beer available, with most restaurants offering at least two or three, and sometimes even five or six options. If you find yourself unsure about the question, don't fret too much. Simply shrug your shoulders, and they will bring you a suitable selection.

The waiter might inform you, "Apologies, we don't have samgyeopsal, but we do have ogyeopsal." Don't be concerned if you were anticipating the former, as "ogyeopsal" signifies that it has five layers of meat instead of three. If the pork belly still retains the skin, it is referred to as ogyeopsal, which tends to be slightly more expensive and chewier compared to samgyeopsal. Simply order ogyeopsal and indulge in its gripping flavor.

Once you've successfully placed your order, the food arrives in a flash. The table will be adorned with a dozen or more plates of different sizes, some of which may hold unfamiliar dishes. Even before the meat you ordered arrives, a variety of dishes that you didn't specifically request will be placed on the table. But fear not, my friend, as this is a hallmark characteristic of Korean cuisine known as "banchan" or side dishes. And the best part? They come at no additional cost, and when you finish them, you'll be offered more. Finish those as well, and the servers will bring you even more to savor.

In Korean restaurants, you won't find forks and knives as the primary utensils. Instead, you'll be provided with spoons and chopsticks. While some travelers may not be accustomed to using chopsticks, many are familiar with them, even if they aren't entirely confident in their skills. It's worth noting that Korean chopsticks are known for being the thinnest among other Asian countries, which may require a bit of adjustment for those not used to them.

At times, even after all on-the-house banchans entirely cover the table, you may not see your spoons and chopsticks on the table. In such cases, it's a good idea to check under the table. You'll often find a rectangular box attached to the underside of the table, which contains a set of spoons and chopsticks for your convenience. This is just one example of the peculiar features you'll encounter in Korean restaurants, reflecting their emphasis on efficiency. We'll delve deeper into these intriguing aspects later.

Despite the pork belly being the same, its preparation can vary across different restaurants. For example, some establishments freeze the pork belly, partially thaw it, slice it thinly, and then grill it, while others use raw meat sliced slightly thicker. The thickness of the meat can also differ from place to place. While most restaurants serve the meat raw and uncooked, some may choose to lightly cook it before allowing customers to finish grilling it at their table. The type of grill employed can also vary, with some restaurants using a thick griddle over the fire, while others opt for a classic grill. Furthermore, the level of involvement from the staff in the grilling process varies, as some restaurants handle the grilling from start to finish, while others leave it entirely to the customers. Lastly, some establishments serve small, bite-sized pieces of meat, while others grill larger chunks as a whole and then cut them with scissors instead of knives. The use of scissors is another characteristic element of Korean restaurant culture.

The presence of a grill at the table results in the generation of smoke during the cooking process. To address this, Korean restaurants incorporate an exceptional hood system that descends from the ceiling and hovers just above the grill. This feature is not commonly found in other countries and is unique to Korean dining establishments. In fact, certain Korean restaurants go as far as employing "state-of-the-art" devices that facilitate the escape of smoke underneath the table, further enhancing the dining experience.

The grilled meat is often accompanied by a diverse array of side dishes, enhancing the overall dining experience. While kimchi, a spicy fermented napa cabbage, remains the most common side dish, you will also commonly encounter Korean salads made with finely chopped green onions and vegetables, all mixed with a secret sauce that bursts with flavors. Another attractive addition is the Korean-style pickle called "jangajji", featuring a range of vegetables pickled in flavorful brine or other sauces.

In addition to the side dishes, the meal is complemented with a variety of raw ingredients such as onions, garlics, mushrooms, and other vegetables, which can be grilled right on the table alongside the meat. This interactive cooking process adds an element of fun to the dining experience. To enhance the flavors further, a wide selection of sauces is available to dip the meat in. Common choices include salt, salt mixed with sesame oil, wasabi, and ssamjang. For those seeking more adventurous flavors, "jeotgal", a salted and fermented seafood-based sauce made from an array of seafood, can also be found.

Alright, it's time to indulge in this mouthwatering, crispy meat! There are plenty of ways to savor the flavors and create your perfect bite. Start by enjoying the meat with just a sprinkle of good old salt to relish its natural taste. Then, explore the various sauces available to elevate the flavors further. Experiment with different combinations, dipping the meat into sauces like ssamjang, sesame oil mixed with salt, or even a touch of fiery wasabi for a kick. To add freshness and texture to each bite, accompany the meat with a side of kimchi or assorted vegetables.

For the ultimate culinary experience, try the favored Korean practice called "ssam". Take a lettuce or perilla leaf, lay it out in your hand, place a piece of meat on top, and add a dollop of ssamjang. Wrap it up tightly and enjoy the explosion of flavors and textures in a single bite. You can simply call it "Korean taco." Remember, ssamjang refers to the sauce (jang) that accompanies the ssam (wrap). Feel free to explore different combinations and discover your preferred way of enjoying this delicious dish.

The flavors of samgyeopsal may take a little getting used to, but once you start relishing its deliciousness, you'll find that the meat disappears quickly. Unless you have a small appetite, I highly recommend to order extra meat to truly indulge in the experience. In Korean restaurants, a unit of meat is typically marketed as a serving size for one person. However, the actual quantity can vary across establishments, ranging from 130 to 150 grams (from 4.5 to 5.3 ounces) or even more. Regardless of the advertised serving size, it's common to find that a single portion of meat is often not enough to satisfy your cravings. (In the United States, a standard serving of steak usually ranges from 8 to 10 ounces.) There's a well-known Korean joke that says, "If it tastes good, it has 0 calories." So, don't hesitate to order more meat to fully enjoy the flavors and make sure you're fully satiated. It's entirely normal for one person to consume 1.5 or even 2 servings of meat during their meal.

Once you've finished enjoying the extra meat, you might think it's time to settle the bill and leave. However, in Korean culture, the dining experience doesn't always end there. If a waiter approaches you and asks if you want more meat, and you decline, they might ask again, "So what would you eat for a meal?"

You might be taken aback by this question, wondering if all the food you've been eating wasn't considered a meal. But in Korean culture, meat alone is not always considered a complete meal. Many Koreans continue their dining experience by ordering additional dishes such as a Korean stew called "kimchi-jjigae" or "doenjang-jjigae", which is enjoyed with rice, or they opt for cold noodles known as "naengmyeon". Jjigae and naengmyeon are indeed significant dishes in Korean cuisine, and we will explore them in more detail later. However, for now, let's move on.

If you're curious about the cost, let me give you an estimate. For a party of two who order three servings of pork belly, a bottle of soju, one jjigae, and one cold noodle dish, you can anticipate a bill of around $50, which may vary slightly depending on the specific restaurant. Unlike in certain countries, there is no tipping culture in Korea, meaning that this is the final price. Considering the generally high cost of living in South Korea, samgyeopsal is quite a bargain.

At the beginning of this article, I emphasized that if someone could only have one meal in Korea, it should be samgyeopsal. However, when you ask Koreans for their recommendation on the ultimate meal for a foreigner, surprisingly, samgyeopsal may not always be the top choice. It's challenging to pinpoint a single answer since, if you were to survey 100 people, you would likely receive at least 10 different responses. So, why did I initially recommend samgyeopsal? The reason goes beyond the food itself. It lies in the complete experience of visiting a Korean restaurant and immersing oneself in Korean food culture.

As previously mentioned, soju is widely regarded as the ideal pairing drink to complement the flavors of pork belly. In an upcoming article, I will explore the rich history and peculiar characteristics of soju.

# 2.
# Soju, the Korean Soul Drink

Although not universally known, there's a good chance you're familiar with soju. Even if you haven't tried it, you've likely encountered it on the screen. If you are perusing this book, it stands to reason that you hold a notable interest in Korea, and as such, it is conceivable that you have been exposed to Korean films or dramas, whether it be the phenomenon of "Squid Game", the acclaimed "Parasite," or perhaps even a lesser-known production.

It's safe to say that almost every Korean movie or drama incorporates soju in some way. While I haven't personally examined each and every one of them, you can bet that soju will make an appearance at least once, unless the story is set before the Korean War. It's just impossible to truly capture the essence of Korean culture without touching on the ubiquitous drink that is soju.

Right from the start of Parasite, as Choi Woo-sik and Park Seo-joon's characters cross paths, they're knocking back shots of soju from those tiny glasses. Yup, that same clear green bottle that's widespread throughout Korea. And in Squid Game, we see Lee Jung-jae and Oh Young-soo indulging in the potent potable while munching on uncooked ramen. (I'll dive deeper into the raw ramen scene in an upcoming piece on the dish.) Interestingly enough, both scenes unfold outside a convenience store, but truth be told, Koreans will tip back soju just about anywhere they can.

Soju, which literally translates to "burned liquor", is a time-honored distilled spirit originating from Korea and has been cherished for centuries, dating back to the 13th century. Traditionally produced by fermenting rice or other grains, this libation boasts a transparent, colorless complexion. Though the alcohol strength can fluctuate, it is not unusual for soju to deliver a potent kick, ranging from 16% to well over 50%.

Correct! Soju falls into the category of distilled spirits. Alcoholic beverages can be broadly classified into two main types: fermented beverages like beer and wine, and distilled beverages such as whiskey and vodka. Distilled spirits undergo a process of distillation, which separates and concentrates the alcohol content, resulting in higher alcohol levels compared to fermented beverages. Due to their production method and increased potency, distilled spirits often come with a higher price tag.

The affordability of soju is a source of wonder for many foreigners. It's astounding how inexpensive it can be. A customary 360 ml bottle can be acquired at a restaurant for approximately $4, while supermarkets and convenience stores often sell it for just a little over a dollar. In fact, when compared globally, soju stands out as one of the most budget-friendly spirits available. (Ironically, what often astonishes foreigners about soju is not its flavor or fragrance, but rather its price.) Now, what's the secret behind its remarkable affordability?

In Korea, there exist two distinct types of soju, each occupying a different price range. The first type encompasses premium or high-end soju, comparable to other costly spirits found worldwide. On the other hand, the second type, which is more prevalent and affordable, is the beloved soju that graces the screens of films and dramas and finds its place in the hearts of Koreans. It's the kind you'll commonly encounter at restaurants throughout Korea. Despite sharing the same name, these two variations of soju diverge in their production techniques and ingredients.

The more expensive, premium soju in Korea is meticulously distilled, offering a refined and signature flavor profile. On the other hand, the widely beloved and affordable variety, recognizable by its iconic green bottles, is known as diluted soju. Diluted soju is created by blending high-proof alcohol with water and incorporating a moderate sweetener, resulting in a remarkably smooth and pleasing taste. (So, soju may or may not be a distilled spirit.) It's worth noting that while the practice of diluting spirits is found in several countries, none have attained the same level of popularity as Korean soju.

Now, I don't want to get all scientific on you because, let's face it, even I'm not entirely sure about all the intricate details. But here's the deal: think of the relationship between distilled and diluted soju like the difference between butter and margarine. I'll refer to the diluted version as 'soju' from here on out, and if I need to mention the distilled kind, I'll call it 'premium soju'.

When did soju attain its widespread acclaim in Korea? Historically, Koreans brewed various types of alcohol at home until the 19th century. However, in the early 20th century, the alcohol industry underwent significant changes as it became heavily regulated and associated with taxation, making it illegal to produce and sell alcohol without a license. This shift gave rise to the emergence of soju companies, and the beverage quickly gained prominence, particularly the more affordable options that appealed to a nation facing economic challenges. During periods of scarcity, such as in the aftermath of the Korean War, laws were even enacted to prohibit the production of rice-based alcohol, further solidifying soju as one of the few available alcoholic beverages for Koreans.

For much of the latter half of the 20th century, soju in Korea commonly had an alcohol content of 25 percent. Its purpose was primarily to facilitate inebriation rather than being savored for its flavor. Even in the present day, Koreans endure grueling work hours, but in the past, their workloads were even more arduous, accompanied by elevated stress levels. Soju served as a quick and affordable means of getting intoxicated, offering a brief respite from the daily grind before returning to work the following morning. The aim was to consume it swiftly, become inebriated rapidly, temporarily escaping life's hardships, and then recuperate at home in preparation for the challenges of the next day's work.

In 1998, the world of soju experienced a breakthrough when one company introduced a 23 percent variant that quickly made a splash among drinkers. The exact reason for its success remains uncertain, whether it was due to a shift in Koreans' daily lives towards a less hectic pace or other factors. Following this, other companies joined the trend by launching their own versions with slightly lower alcohol content. As a result, the majority of Korean soju available today features an alcohol content ranging from approximately 16 to 18 percent.

The consumption of soju in South Korea is nothing short of staggering, with an estimated 4 billion bottles consumed annually. Each bottle generally holds 360 ml of this beloved spirit. Considering the adult population of approximately 40 million, it means that, on average, each adult consumes nearly 100 bottles of soju per year. It's intriguing to note that statistical data suggests Koreans indulge in soju approximately twice a week, typically savoring one bottle during each drinking session.

Contrary to the common perception of Korean people, statistics indicate that Koreans do not have a particularly high alcohol consumption rate compared to other OECD countries. However, it is important to note that Koreans have a lower tolerance for alcohol due to their genetics. Approximately 30% of Koreans are genetically predisposed to have limited levels of the enzymes required to break down alcohol, making it challenging for them to consume even small amounts without experiencing adverse effects such as facial flushing and headaches. This genetic condition is also prevalent in Japan and China. Considering these figures, it wouldn't be unfounded to suggest that the remaining 70% of Koreans exhibit considerable enthusiasm when it comes to their drinking habits.

To embark on your soju journey, I recommend starting with the iconic green-bottled soju, which proudly holds the title of South Korea's national drink. You can find it everywhere, from restaurants to convenience stores, and it's even allowed to be consumed in public places like parks, beaches, and streets. South Korea boasts a liberal drinking culture, allowing you to enjoy your soju in a multitude of settings, unless expressly prohibited. When it comes to food pairings, soju is known to harmonize well with almost anything, according to the Korean palate. However, to be honest, it tends to find its truest match with salty, spicy delicacies, and fatty dishes like pork belly.

When you take your first sip of soju, you might find it surprising and unfamiliar to your taste buds. It lacks a pronounced flavor or aroma, almost resembling a diluted blend of ethanol. However, as you continue to indulge, you may detect a subtle sweetness that stems from a mysterious sweetener. While some global wanderers appreciate the novelty of this singular libation, for many foreigners, soju is simply an average drink, especially during travel to Korea, that offers affordability. Let's be honest, soju may not be considered one of the most extraordinary beverages in the world. Nevertheless, it's undeniable that this inexpensive elixir carries immense cultural importance for Koreans.

To start with, soju is widely regarded as a drink for the "average Korean Joe". High-ranking officials, CEOs, and famous personalities are often photographed drinking soju intentionally to appear more down to earth. In Korean social dynamics, responding to the question of your preferred drink with wine or whiskey, especially for men, might lead to being perceived as pretentious. (Of course, not always.) To maintain a friendly atmosphere and avoid any potential misinterpretation, it's often considered wise to respond with soju regardless of your actual preference. Similarly, when someone suggests, "Let's drink soju sometime," it often carries an underlying message of wanting to deepen the connection and get to know each other better.

The choice of drink can also convey subtly different social meanings in Korea. For instance, inviting a friend to "have a beer" is often seen as a casual social activity, while asking to "have a soju" may indicate a desire to confide or release pent-up emotions. The latter expression can sometimes imply a more serious or even melancholic tone, as if to say "I need to forget about my troubles for a while, so let's drink together."

In Korea, soju serves as a unique unit of measurement when it comes to discussing one's alcohol consumption. It's interesting to note that asking "How much can you drink?" is not a common question in many other countries, but in Korea, it's almost a customary greeting. Whether you're interacting with coworkers, friends, new acquaintances, or even having a job interview, it's not uncommon for the topic of alcohol tolerance or drinking capacity, known as "juryang" in Korean, to come up.

When asked about their drinking capacity, people in Korea

often measure it in terms of bottles of soju. (If they mention just number of bottles, it automatically refers to soju.) It's worth noting that in Korean culture, drinking capacity is often regarded as a way to compete, especially among men. It is not uncommon for individuals to exaggerate their drinking ability as a means to showcase their resilience and social prowess. Notably, in certain professions, being known as a 'big drinker' can even provide an advantage during the hiring process.

Soju can certainly be enjoyed on its own, but it is also frequently mixed with beer to create a refreshing cocktail called "somaek". The common ratio is approximately 1 part soju to 3 parts beer. While somaek is not commonly found at bars, mastering the art of mixing it to the right proportions can earn you praise from your friends, even though you shouldn't expect tipping for your mixing skills. This combination is particularly appealing for those who find straight soju too strong or not so attractive. Mixing a small amount of affordable soju with a regular beer can create the illusion of a 'premium beer' with higher alcohol content.

To foreigners, the taste of soju might all taste the same, but to Koreans, it can vary depending on the brand. Actually, many

Koreans have a preferred brand of soju and can discern the differences between brands even in a blind taste test. As a result, it is common for most restaurants in Korea to offer a selection of at least three different types of soju for customers to choose from. When ordering soju at a restaurant, servers may ask you to specify which brand you would like, which can be challenging if you're not familiar with Korean. Fortunately, there is a handy Korean phrase to know: "Amugona!" which means "Anything is OK."

If you're looking to add a touch of humor to your drink order, you can try shouting "Tesla!" This might seem peculiar since it's the name of an electric car, but it's actually a well-known joke among Koreans. When you order a 'Tesla' at a restaurant, you'll be served an amusing combination of beverages: a bottle of Terra, a Korean beer, and a bottle of "Chamisul" soju. (The name 'Tesla' comes from combining 'Te' from Terra and 'sul' from Chamisul. Why the 'a' is added? Don't ask. It's a playful wordplay.) The server will bring your order without further questions, though they may be curious how a foreigner is aware of this inside joke. Chamisul is a widely recognized brand that has been a favorite for nearly a century and holds the distinction of being the 'best-selling distilled spirit in the world'. It's worth noting that Chamisul alone sells nearly 2 billion bottles annually, including exports.

When you order a Tesla, you'll be presented with two different glasses. Begin by savoring the soju on its own from a small glass, appreciating its own flavor. Then, in the larger glass, combine the soju with beer to create a refreshing concoction known as somaek, which offers a glimpse into Korean drinking scene. It's important to note that not all soju brands come in green glass bottles; some are packaged in clear glass, so don't be surprised if you're served soju in a clear bottle.

If you have a few extra days in Korea and are willing to splurge, I recommend exploring the world of premium soju. While it may come at a higher price, both in restaurants and convenience stores, the experience is well worth it. These premium varieties, which can cost five to ten times more than regular soju, offer an alcohol content of around 40 percent, providing a considerably stronger kick. The taste of premium soju is difficult to capture in words, but it exudes a sense of luxury. Crafted using traditional methods, it embodies the essence of a true spirit and can be likened to a Korean interpretation of whiskey. Notable premium soju brands to consider include Hwayo, Ilpoom Jinro, and Andong Soju.

# 3.

# The Hustle and
# Bustle of Seoul

Excluding North Korea, South Korea has an area of approximately 100,000 square kilometers (38,600 square miles) and is ranked 107th in the world for land area. Although not a very small country itself, it pales in comparison to the size of Canada, the United States, and China, being only a little over one hundredth of their size. Russia, the world's largest country, is 170 times the size of South Korea. (Korea isn't too small, it's just that Russia is too big.) South Korea is roughly one-fifth the size of Spain and one-third the size of Italy. Some countries with similar areas include Cuba, Iceland, Hungary, and Portugal.

Despite its small land area, South Korea is home to around

50 million people, making it one of the most densely populated countries in the world. With a population density of just over 500 people per square kilometer, it ranks second only to Bangladesh among countries with over 10 million inhabitants and first among OECD countries. These figures indicate that South Korea has a considerable population living in a compact area.

Notably, a staggering 72% of South Korea's overall land area is mountainous. While other countries also have high proportions of mountainous regions, most of South Korea's mountains are incredibly steep and rugged, making it challenging to build and develop in those areas. As a result, South Korea's population is even more tightly packed than Bangladesh, which has mostly flat terrain.

For comparison's sake, countries like Cuba, Hungary, and Portugal, which are comparable in size to South Korea, have population densities of 100 to 110 people per square kilometer, which is around one-fifth of South Korea's density. While Iceland is known for its isolation, it's still worth noting that its population density is only 3.6 people per square kilometer, which is lower than both Russia and Canada but slightly higher than Australia. This means that 150 Koreans occupy the same space as one person in Iceland or Australia.

Moreover, the congestion in South Korea's capital city, Seoul, is simply overwhelming. With 10 million residents, which accounts for 20% of the country's population, squeezed into an area of just 600 square kilometers (231 square miles), the population density in Seoul alone exceeds 16,000 people per square kilometer. To put it another way, Seoul's population density is over double that of Singapore (7,600) or Hong Kong (6,500). While there are cities in countries like Bangladesh and India that are more densely populated than Seoul, it's evident that Seoul is one of the most densely populated and crowded cities in the world. Notably, Seoul even has a quarter of its land area covered by mountains.

The surrounding areas of Seoul are equally packed with people. Gyeonggi Province, which encircles Seoul, is home to around 13 million individuals, while Incheon Metropolitan City, which is not far from Seoul (and is where Incheon International Airport is located), has approximately 3 million inhabitants. Collectively, Seoul, Gyeonggi, and Incheon are often known as the "capital area," indicating that over half of South Korea's population resides in this region alone.

South Korea is not a city-state like Singapore, and even though it has a substantial number of mountains, 100,000 square kilometers is not a small area. Therefore, one might wonder why the population is concentrated in a specific area instead of being spread out across the country. While there is some historical context to this phenomenon, we will delve into it later.

Regardless, with such a densely populated city, there are many aspects of Seoul that may appear unfamiliar to outsiders. Firstly, it's worth noting that Koreans are accustomed to residing in relatively smaller personal spaces.

Cultural norms regarding personal space can vary significantly from one society to another and even between individuals. In Western culture, for example, people often feel comfortable standing at least three meters away from complete strangers. Even between casual acquaintances, it is customary to maintain a distance of at least a meter or more, while conversations with close friends and family usually take place at a distance of around half a meter.

Living in densely populated cities in Korea, it becomes challenging to maintain such distances. However, Koreans also appreciate open spaces and secluded areas with fewer people, and when they go on vacation, they often seek out less crowded destinations. Despite this, due to the experience of living in densely populated cities, they have grown accustomed to close proximity with others, so they don't feel excessively inconvenienced or anxious about it.

Koreans have a different concept of personal space. When standing in line, Koreans tend to stand near the person in front of them, sometimes less than a meter apart. Long lines can form with only 50 centimeters of space between individuals. (Considering this, it's amazing how well Koreans have been able to maintain social distancing during the coronavirus pandemic.) Koreans believe that each person has a very small allotted space, and it's not that they are insensitive to invading other people's spaces.

To continue, in many crowded situations in Korea, such as on the streets, in markets, on the subway, and in museums, physical contact between people is unavoidable. Koreans have adapted to these situations and are generally comfortable with passing touches, not feeling the need to apologize or expect an apology for them. Unlike in France where people may say 'pardon' when their bodies come close without actually touching, Koreans do not have such a practice. If Koreans were to follow this custom like the French do, subway commuters in Korea might find themselves saying 'pardon' hundreds of times a day, and being tardy for work.

Due to the reasons mentioned earlier, Koreans tend to avoid initiating greetings, making eye contact, or smiling at others in confined spaces like elevators. With a crowd of 17 people in an elevator, it would be nearly impossible to acknowledge each person individually. Koreans may also feel uneasy if a stranger attempts to start a conversation in an elevator, fearing that the person may be a weirdo.

As a foreigner traveling to Korea, don't jump to the conclusion that Koreans are a bunch of boorish space invaders who don't apologize when they bump into you. Koreans are just like you, worn out by the hustle and bustle of big cities and craving for some peace and quiet in a serene locale, perhaps a remote beach in the Mediterranean or a tranquil island in the South Pacific, if they can afford it. Koreans also relish the luxury of having ample personal space, be it on a flight or in a fancy restaurant where tables aren't crammed together like sardines in a can.

By any chance, if you're eager to get a genuine taste of the vibrant energy of Seoul, then why not brave the subway during the rush hour? At roughly 8 in the morning, regardless of which station you hop on at, the train is bound to be crammed to the rafters. And if you're the type of person who loves the thrill of living on the edge, I highly recommend you give Line 9 a try. This line has two options: the "all-stop" and the "express", and trust me, you want to opt for the express. According to a recent survey, this particular line is a whopping 234% over capacity during peak hours. Just let that sink in for a moment. That means a train designed to accommodate 158 passengers will instead be crammed with a staggering 360 passengers. Yikes! Can you imagine?

Sindorim Station, where Line 1 and Line 2 meet; Gangnam Station, where Line 2 and Bundang Line meet (yes, the same Gangnam from Gangnam Style); Sadang Station, where Line 2 and Line 4 meet; Express Terminal Station, where Line 3, 7, and 9 meet; and Dongdaemun History and Culture Park Station, where Line 2, 4, and 5 meet, are other great subway stations for the "congestion experience". If you live in one of the world's many metropolitan cities, you won't need to do this, but if you're a traveler from Iceland or a small town in Australia or Canada, it's worth a try. Don't think the chaos is limited to the morning commute either—evening rush hour is just as packed, if not more so.

Well, here's some good news: you won't have to constantly check your pockets for sneaky pickpockets in South Korea, despite the crowds. Back in the day, these culprits were rampant. I did some digging in the archives and discovered that back in the 80s, one department store in South Korea had to deal with a whopping 50 pickpockets a day. But these days, the game has changed. The number of pickpocketing crimes has gone down to a measly 500 a year in the country. (Besides, more than half of those sneaky thieves get caught. The arrest rate for pickpockets in South Korea is around 60%.) South Korea's low pickpocketing rates can be attributed to its near-complete transition to a cashless society. The majority of South Koreans use credit cards or SmartPay for their daily purchases, with only a handful of elderly folks still hanging onto cash. Even something as small as a cup of coffee or a water bottle can be purchased with a swipe of a card, and cash is seldom seen at eateries or hair salons. Since there's no physical money to pinch, pickpockets in South Korea have been forced to hang up their thieving hats.

You may be questioning if pickpockets in South Korea go beyond just stealing your cash and target your fancy handbag, watch, or smartphone. Well, let me tell you, the country has implemented robust security measures. With loads of CCTV cameras in almost every nook and cranny, and every adult's face and fingerprints on file with the government, the direct theft of cash or goods is pretty darn low. Sure, there are a few tech-based crimes like voice phishing and smishing, but as a foreign tourist, you don't have to stress about that. Worst-case scenario, you may encounter some overpriced goods, but that's not a common occurrence anymore.

Because of the low incidence of theft in public places, South Korea is a great place to relax and not worry about losing your personal belongings. For instance, if you need to step away from your laptop, phone, or wallet at a Starbucks, you can do so without concern or asking strangers to watch your belongings. You can leave your belongings unattended when you go to the bathroom or step out for a smoke. Many young people even study and work in cafes with their belongings unguarded. If you accidentally leave your phone or wallet at a restaurant, there's no need to panic. Just head back to the restaurant and the owner will likely have taken care of it, or it might still be where you left it if it's a quiet time of day.

If you happen to visit a subway station near a baseball stadium on game day in Korea, you'll witness a pretty bizarre sight. Although most subway stations have coin lockers, there are only about a hundred or so available, which isn't nearly enough to accommodate the tens of thousands of spectators that arrive at the same time. So what do fans do with luggage that's too big to bring into the packed ballpark? Well, the answer is simple: they can just leave it "near" the lockers and come back for it after the game. No joke. And get this—there's no storage fee since it's just out in the open. On busy game days, the number of bags left unattended can reach into the hundreds.

In South Korea, there's no escaping the watchful eye of CCTV cameras. With over 1.3 million cameras installed by public institutions, it's evident that extensive surveillance is in place. While this number may not be as high as in China, it's still growing at an alarming rate—in just the past decade, they've added a whopping 1 million cameras! Additionally, it is worth noting that South Korea boasts an estimated 7 million privately installed CCTVs within the country. In fact, a 2011 survey found that citizens in the Seoul metropolitan area were captured on CCTV an average of 83 times a day, and with the number of cameras increasing rapidly every year, that number is likely even higher now. So, unless you're exceptionally adept at avoiding surveillance, assume that you're being recorded hundreds of times each day.

It is also worth noting that an astonishing 90% of all cars in South Korea have dash cameras installed. With around 25 million cars in the country, that translates to over 20 million dash cameras on the road. Consequently, Koreans are leaving a constant trail or trace, whether they are traveling on foot or in a vehicle.

South Korea may seem like a society where every move you make is being monitored, creating a footprint of your activities through credit cards, CCTVs, smartphones, and the internet, with data being stored for a period of time. Despite this, there is not much public concern about the idea of "Big Brother" in Korea. While issues of privacy and invasion of privacy do arise, the majority view seems to be that more security technology is needed to better protect sensitive and important information. Perhaps this is due to South Korea's status as a global leader in information and communication technology.

There is one more behavior in Korea that is influenced by its historical and cultural context. In contrast to the Western practice of holding doors for others, this behavior is not as common in Korea. This could be due to two possible reasons. Firstly, the high population density in Korea means that people often stand close together and pass through doors quickly without requiring someone to hold the door for them. Secondly, traditional Korean architecture often includes sliding doors that move left and right, although swing doors that move back and forth are also used. This means that the person behind won't be hit by a moving door, even if the person in front doesn't care. Therefore, travelers from the West should be aware and cautious when passing through a door in Korea to avoid being hit by a swing door.

Koreans are basically nice and friendly people, which holds particularly true for foreign tourists. While they might not always say sorry if they accidentally bump into you or hold the door out of consideration for the person behind, you can still expect a warm reception and hospitality during your stay in Korea. So, bon voyage and enjoy your time in this welcoming country!

# 4.

# Seoul Subway: The Best in the World

The Seoul subway system never fails to amaze foreigners. While other big cities may boast subways of their own, Seoul's is truly something special. Not only does it have an impressive number of lines and stations, but the fares are also incredibly affordable. You can ride to your heart's content without breaking the bank! But that's not all—the system is known for its exceptional cleanliness and fresh air, thanks to the screen doors that line almost every station. And to top it all off, there's free Wi-Fi for commuters to stay connected.

It's a fact that Seoul was not the first city to build a subway system. London, England, holds that title with the first underground railway constructed way back in 1863. The United States joined the subway club in 1898 when Boston built its first subway system. Buenos Aires, Argentina, became the pioneer in Latin America, opening its subway system in 1913, while Tokyo, Japan, took the lead in Asia with its subway system established in 1927. Surprisingly, Seoul didn't join the subway train until 1974, a striking 111 years after London! Among Asian cities, Seoul was the fourth to develop a subway system, following Tokyo, Beijing (in 1969), and Pyongyang (in 1973). Interestingly, Pyongyang had a head start, opening its subway system in 1973, a year before Seoul. Meanwhile, the African continent had to wait until 1987, when Cairo built its first subway system.

Railroads have been a part of South Korea's transportation infrastructure since 1899, but the development of a subway system was a much later endeavor. There are several reasons why Seoul's subway system was built so late. Firstly, Korea was a latecomer to modernization, and its capital, Seoul, didn't experience marked population growth until the mid-20th century. While Seoul's population had been steadily increasing since it surpassed the 1 million mark in 1942, the Korean War, which began in 1950, substantially disrupted the city's growth. By the end of the war,

Seoul's population still hovered around 1 million.

Since the Korean War ended, Seoul's population explosion began. Just six years after the war ended, in 1959, the population had already doubled to over 2 million. From then on, the city's population continued to swell at an incredible pace, growing by 1 million every two to five years. By 1988, Seoul's population had finally surpassed 10 million. This astonishing growth meant that it took only 35 years for Seoul to transform from a city of 1 million to a megacity of 10 million. (During that period, due to the changes in administrative zones, Seoul's area was also enlarged, contributing to its population explosion.)

When London constructed its first subway in 1863, the city had a population of approximately 2.5 million with GDP per capita of around $3,000. In contrast, during the 1950s, South Korea was still grappling with significant economic challenges as one of the poorest nations, and Seoul's population was less than two million. Consequently, the financial capacity to invest in infrastructure projects like the subway was limited. Even as the population surged and traffic congestion became problematic in the 1960s, concrete plans for a subway system remained vague, primarily due to a lack of available resources. It wasn't until 1969 that South Korea's GDP per capita reached $200, although the country still faced persistent poverty. (It's unclear when South Korea's GDP per capita crossed the $100 mark, as accurate statistics weren't available, but experts estimate it to be in the early 1960s.)

Before the subway was built, Seoul had a public transportation system that mainly relied on buses and streetcars. Cars were only owned by a small number of wealthy people and taxis were not commonly used. As the population increased, traffic congestion worsened and the city eventually made the decision to discontinue the streetcars and construct a subway. From the cessation of the streetcars in 1968 until the opening of the first subway line in 1974, Seoul was notorious for its heavy traffic, and was called "traffic hell".

The construction of the Seoul subway began in 1970, overcoming a multitude of challenges, and culminated in the successful inauguration of Line 1 on August 15, 1974. Despite its initial length of only 7.8 kilometers and 10 stations, Line 1 played a pivotal role in connecting two of the most important stations in Seoul: Seoul Station and Cheongnyangni Station. Notably, these two stations served as crucial transportation hubs for trains departing from Seoul to other regions of the country.

Additionally, during the construction of Subway Line 1, some of the existing railway tracks were double-tracked, effectively extending the length and scope of the subway line.

The opening of Subway Line 1 generated significant anticipation among the residents of Seoul, leading to the planning of a grand opening ceremony that would be graced by the president. Interestingly, the chosen opening date of August 15th held special importance as it coincided with South Korea's most notable national holiday, National Liberation Day. South Korea had endured 35 years of colonial rule until August 15, 1945, marking the only period of colonization in its extensive history spanning thousands of years.

However, during the National Liberation Day ceremony preceding the subway opening, a momentous incident unfolded. A tragic assassination attempt on the president occurred, resulting in the unfortunate death of the first lady. The assailant was identified as a Korean-Japanese communist, although the extent of his connections to North Korea remained undisclosed.

Seoul has been under construction ever since, with the building of subway lines 2, 3, and 4 taking place almost simultaneously. Line 2 opened in 1980, followed by Lines 3 and 4 in

1985. However, by 1985, the population of Seoul had already neared 10 million, and four subway lines were insufficient. Despite this, the construction of the subway system was put on hold for a while due to a much bigger and more important event on the horizon: the 1988 Seoul Olympics.

During the 1970s and 1980s, South Korea experienced a rapid pace of development. The GDP per capita surpassed $200 in 1969, $400 in 1973, $600 in 1975, $800 in 1976, and finally $1,000 in 1977. By 1983, just six years later, it had exceeded $2,000, and by 1987 it had crossed $3,000. In 1988, when the Seoul Olympics were held in a developing country for the first time, South Korea's GDP per capita reached $4,755. This economic transformation is often referred to as the "Miracle on the Han River."

After the devastation of the Korean War, South Korea was left in ruins. However, it was a truly remarkable achievement that within a span of just 35 years, the nation had undergone such rapid development that it was able to host the Olympics. This was not only surprising to the rest of the world, but also to Koreans themselves, who wondered whether such a feat was even possible. During the late 1970s and early 1980s, when the effort to bid to host the Olympics was being made, few Koreans believed it could be accomplished. Even the more optimistic among them thought that if they failed this time, they could use the experience to their advantage and perhaps host the Olympics in 1996 or 2000.

There's a German city that every Korean over the age of 50 knows. It's called Baden-Baden. Now, don't go thinking everyone knows where the heck it is - truth is, most folks haven't got a clue where it is! But, why does it matter, you ask? Well, let me tell you - it's where the host city for the 1988 Summer Olympics was announced on September 30, 1981. Since the announcement, for years, "Olympics" was the buzzword on everyone's lips, and it seemed like the fate of the entire country was riding on the success of those Games. South Korea went all-in, pulling out all the stops to make sure it was a roaring success.

They built the "Olympic Highway," a brand new urban expressway stretching from Gimpo Airport (back when Incheon Airport wasn't even a thing yet) all the way to the Olympic main stadium. They even cleared out run-down shacks that might've made foreign visitors turn up their noses, and evicted the city's poorest residents. Unfortunately, the construction of the stadiums and athletes' villages led to a huge wave of forced evictions - in fact, the Seoul Games had the highest number of evictions in Olympic history, a record that was only broken years later by the Beijing Games in 2008. To avoid any hint of military tension between North and South Korea, they kept all military personnel and vehicles out of the city, creating an atmosphere of absolute safety and security. When it came to ensuring the success of the Olympics, nothing was off the table.

Believe it or not, subway construction in Seoul actually came to a screeching halt for a bit. One reason was that the budget was already stretched thin after pouring so much cash into preparing for the Olympics. But, there was also a concern that ripping up major roads to build the subway would be "aesthetically unpleasant" (we've all got our priorities, right?). So, work on the subway system didn't resume until 1990, well after the Olympics had come and gone. Line 5 wasn't even up and running until 1995 - a full decade after Line 4 was completed! After that, it was a slow but steady process: Line 7 and 8 opened in 1996, Line 6 in 2000, Line 9 in 2009. Oh, and fun fact - the Seoul Subway lines are numbered according to the order they were planned, not the order they were finished!

But wait, there's more! The nine numbered lines are just the beginning. There are a few more lines with fancy names instead of numbers, and even more that run throughout the greater metropolitan area just beyond Seoul's borders. And, there are still more lines currently under construction or in the planning stages. As of 2022, the entire metropolitan rail system (including Seoul) spans an impressive 23 lines, stretching over 1,262 kilometers and featuring a staggering 640 stations. But, let's be real - these numbers are always in flux. Who knows what kind of new lines and stations they'll have by the time you get there?

Back in the day, the Seoul subway system was infamously dubbed the "Hell Railway". Why? Well, "underground (ji-ha)" and "hell (ji-ok)" are only one letter apart in Korean. And while it's still pretty crowded during peak hours, it was much worse in the past. So much so that subway stations had "pushmen" assigned at every major platform. Yes, you read that right. These pushmen's sole job was to physically shove more passengers into an already-packed train. (Talk about a tough gig. Believe it or not, this was a real thing from the mid-80s all the way up to the mid-2000s. (Japan was the only other country with this kind of job, by the way.) I said it before. Koreans don't apologize if they bump into a stranger. It's just the way things are.

Fortunately, the situation has improved dramatically in recent years, and the current Seoul subway is actually quite efficient. While some lines may still get pretty crowded during rush hour, for the most part, it's a relatively smooth ride. How did things get better? There are two primary reasons why the subway is less crowded now than it used to be.

The first reason is that while Seoul's population has remained steady at around 10 million for the past three decades, the subway network has expanded substantially. It's not just that there are more lines, but that existing lines have been continuously extended. For example, Line 4 had 24 stations and was 28.9 kilometers long when it first opened in 1985, but it has since been steadily extended on both ends, and now includes 52 stations and covers 86.6 kilometers. Similarly, Line 3 has doubled in length and number of stations compared to when it first opened. This trend is also true for other lines, although many of the extensions are located outside of Seoul.

Secondly, the number of cars in Seoul has extensively increased over the years. In 1988, there were only 780,000 cars registered, but that number grew to over 2 million by 1995 and over 3 million by 2014. That's a lot of people choosing to commute by car instead of the subway. And while that might seem like good news for anyone riding the rails, it's not all sunshine and rainbows. Because with all those extra cars on the road, the traffic situation in Seoul has gone from bad to worse. The city's tried to fix the problem by lengthening and widening its roads, but it's just not keeping up with the demand. So, if you're stuck in gridlock during your visit to Seoul, don't worry. You're not witnessing a big event or rally, nor a major car accident, but rather just experiencing an ordinary day in Seoul.

One of the remarkable advantages of the Seoul subway is its convenience. Almost all Koreans utilize a "transportation card" to pay for their subway fares, which is either a prepaid or post-paid system linked to their credit cards. The transport card is not only used for the subway, but also for buses and taxis. The subway also boasts a top-notch air conditioning and heating system that ensures comfortable temperatures all year round. In fact, during the hot summer months, there are even carriages equipped with both stronger and weaker air conditioning to cater to everyone's preferences.

The Seoul subway also offers special seating arrangements

for those who need them. Elderly and disabled individuals have designated seats, as do pregnant women, marked with pink-colored seats. It's a cultural norm to avoid sitting in these seats even when they're empty. As previously mentioned, the subway provides free Wi-Fi for passengers. It's worth noting that despite this amenity, few Koreans opt to use subway Wi-Fi as many have cell phone plans with generous amounts of high-speed internet service, such as LTE or 5G. For those accustomed to lightning-fast internet, subway Wi-Fi can be a frustratingly slow alternative.

The Seoul subway system is a steal with its affordable fares. You can travel almost anywhere within the city for just one dollar. Even if you ride for an hour straight, it's still just a dollar. There are no additional fees for transfers, with the rare exception of a few lines. For longer journeys, the price may go up a little. If you want to save money and add some adventure to your trip, why not combine your subway ride with a city bus? You can transfer between buses and subways without any additional cost. So even if you have to take a bus to the subway station and transfer twice to reach your destination, it's still only a dollar. (When riding a bus, it's crucial to tap your transportation card on the sensor both when boarding and disembarking. This is especially important if you plan to transfer to the subway, as failure to do so may result in extra charges. So, don't forget to tap your card, when you get off the bus at your stop!)

If you are 65 years or older (and a Korean citizen), you can ride the Seoul subway for free regardless of how far or how often you use it, although city buses still require payment. This policy has been in place since 1984, and it reflects the respect that Korean culture places on the elderly. However, it was also implemented in part by a president who was struggling with low approval ratings and sought to win public support.

Due to its low fares and free rides for citizens over 65, the Seoul subway often operates at a loss, with deficits of up to a billion dollars per year being common. Although politicians seeking reelection are reluctant to increase fares, keeping public transportation prices low is a way to make up for a welfare system that is still relatively weak compared to the size of the country's economy.

Seoul's taxi fares are relatively low compared to other countries due to similar reasons as the subway fares. The government effectively sets the taxi fares, and they are one-third to one-fifth the cost of large cities in the United States, Europe, and Japan.

The government subsidizes privately run bus and taxi companies to keep the prices low, just like the subway's deficit is covered by taxes.

The issue of raising subway fares, increasing taxi fares, and eliminating free rides for people over 65 is a constant debate in South Korea. Some people who rarely use the subway argue that it is unfair for their taxes to pay for the fares of other subway riders. However, others believe that affordable public transportation is essential to ensure that low-income people and the elderly have access to transportation. The debate over transportation fares reflects a larger political and social debate about the role of government in society and the balance between individual responsibility and social welfare.

Attention, fellow travelers! While the public transportation fare debates in South Korea continue, you have the perfect opportunity to enjoy the incredible affordability of getting around Seoul. Exploring the city for an entire day won't break the bank. Unless you're a jet-setting high roller, it's unlikely you'll spend more than $10 on subway fares alone. Even if you opt for a taxi ride or two, your total transportation expenses will likely be around $30 to $40. So why not make the most of these fantastic deals and take advantage of the low-cost transportation options while you have the chance? (Spend the transportation savings on food.)

Foreign tourists in Seoul can also take advantage of special tickets, but beware that they may not be the best value. These tickets are available in different durations, ranging from 1 to 7 days, but to truly benefit from the discount, you would need to ride the subway or bus at least 10 times a day. Unless you plan to break a world record for riding the subway, it's probably not worth it. Take your time, immerse yourself in the city, and savor the experience. Seoul has transformed from a "traffic hell" to a "traffic paradise," especially for foreign travelers.

# 5.

# Enjoy Your Chimaek
# at the Ballpark

On October 26, 2019, I had the incredible opportunity to fulfill one of my lifelong dreams. I was fortunate enough to be present at the ballpark, where I cheered passionately as the Doosan Bears secured victory in the Korean Series. This was a moment I had been eagerly anticipating for 38 years, ever since professional baseball debuted in Korea back in 1982. Let me tell you, my friends, it was an exhilarating and nerve-wracking game from start to finish.

The score swung back and forth throughout the game, with the early inning showing a score of 3-8, then turning into a thrilling comeback at 9-8, and ultimately resulting in a tie at 9-9 by the bottom of the ninth inning. However, in the gripping extra innings, the Bears managed to take the lead and emerged as the champions with a final score of 11-9. I must confess, tears of joy streamed down my face at that victorious moment.

Every devoted sports fan understands that winning a championship like the Korean Series is no easy feat. It requires immense determination, resilience, and a bit of luck. Not only is winning challenging, but acquiring tickets for such highly anticipated events can also be equally arduous due to the intense competition. (As I revisited the captivating highlights of the game while composing this post, the euphoria I felt at that moment resurfaced once again.)

I'm a huge fan of sports, with baseball being my absolute favorite. But I also enjoy watching soccer and a variety of other sports. While watching games on TV can be entertaining, there's nothing quite like the exhilaration that comes from being there in person. Admittedly, watching sports at the stadium can come with its share of discomforts - no commentary, no replays, no close-ups, and you're even exposed to the elements like heat, cold, and rain. However, there's a unique sense of atmosphere and energy that you can only experience firsthand at a stadium.

I find that this inclination towards experiencing games myself extends to my travels, and I frequently seek out stadiums in foreign countries as part of my itinerary.

During my inaugural trip abroad to Paris, France, I had the opportunity to attend a sporting spectacle at the iconic Parc des Princes, the hallowed grounds of Paris Saint-Germain FC. (This is the team that South Korean player Lee Kang-in has been playing for since 2023.) Without a specific allegiance to any team, my focus naturally gravitated towards the stadium itself and the spirited crowd rather than the players or the game unfolding on the pitch. The PSG supporters left an indelible impression on me, their synchronized foot-stomping creating an exhilarating rhythm that sent shivers down my spine. As I absorbed the electric atmosphere, a fleeting concern crossed my mind that the venerable structure, which traces its roots back to 1897, might struggle to withstand the unbridled fervor of the passionate fans.

Then, being a novice on my initial journey, I possessed limited knowledge. However, as my travels unfolded, I was fortunate to partake in sporting spectacles across a multitude of nations. From Italy and England to the Netherlands, the United States, Japan, Australia, and Thailand, each stadium experience showcased a distinctive ambiance that served as a true reflection of the country itself. It became apparent to me that, in my opinion, the collective energy of the crowd and the stadium culture encapsulated the very essence and character of the nation at large.

During my visit to Italy, I had the opportunity to attend an AS Roma home game, with the legendary Francesco Totti leading the team as captain. From the moment I arrived at the stadium, the atmosphere was boisterous, with firecrackers exploding, smoke in the air, adding to the charged ambience. The stadium was heavily guarded, with a strong police presence and firefighters equipped with hoses, creating an unusual sight.

Once the game kicked off, the intensity reached another level entirely. The deafening roar of the crowd reverberated through the stands, making it feel as though a riot could break out at any moment. The passionate fans shouted and jeered with fervor, their voices echoing in every direction. It was a sight to behold, amidst occasional objects being flung across the stands and some spectators even attempting to climb the fences. Here, someone was fighting, there, someone was running. What struck me the most was that this was not a cup final or a particularly significant match - it was just an average game.

AS Roma initially held a two-goal lead, but eventually con-
ceded an equalizer and then fell behind midway through the
second half. The stadium erupted, or rather, the crowd did. But
surprisingly, many people began to leave with still more than 10
minutes left on the clock. I couldn't understand why they were
leaving, especially when the game was far from over. As Yogi
Berra once said, it ain't over till it's over. What the heck are they
even doing? As time went on, more and more people continued
to leave, which made me wonder what they were rushing to see
outside. Were they hoping to get better seats to yell at the players? Should I also leave and see what was happening? It was a
tough decision, but in the end, I stood up with five minutes left
to see what was going to happen next.

The area surrounding the stadium was an absolute disaster.
Massive throngs of people, hordes of motorcycles, and streets
already packed with cars. The reason they bailed before the final
whistle was surprisingly straightforward. If they hung around
too long, they'd be snarled in traffic for hours. That's right.
Italians are wild about soccer, but I thought they hate waiting
almost as much as they love soccer.

The stadium's location on the outskirts of Rome posed challenges for transportation, with narrow and congested roads making it difficult to access. Rome's subway system is limited due to the presence of historical ruins, which complicates construction. (Rome is a really cool city, but when it comes to subways, it doesn't quite measure up to Seoul.) I found myself waiting for over 20 minutes for a bus and then enduring another 20 minutes navigating through the crowded streets near the stadium. Those who bailed early traded the chance of witnessing an equalizer or an upset for avoiding a traffic nightmare.

During my business trip to Amsterdam, Netherlands, I visited Ajax's home stadium. To my surprise, the most remarkable aspect wasn't the game, the stadium, or the crowd, but the concession stands. I was initially puzzled when I realized I couldn't make a purchase with cash or credit cards, while everyone around me was happily enjoying their hot dogs and beers. I wondered how they managed to buy their food. It turns out that Ajax only accepts payments through a reloadable prepaid card featuring their logo. I went to the top-up station and loaded 30 euros onto the card, carefully calculating the cost of the food I wanted to buy. (There were four of us; I didn't eat alone.) Since I wouldn't be returning anytime soon, I didn't need to add too much. In the end, I spent €29 and had €1 left over, but it was worth it for the souvenir of that pretty Ajax card. (It's worth mentioning that this happened over ten years ago when the Netherlands was already embracing a cashless society.)

I have to say, the idea of having a prepaid card system for easy payments was a stroke of genius for a highly commercialized country like the Netherlands. No more long lines or fumbling for cash, plus they can earn interest on any leftover funds. And let's not forget about the potential big bucks from all those unused small amounts, like the change I left on my Ajax card. On a side note, the Dutch fans are also pretty chill with their support. None of that screaming and cheering at random, they keep it cool and only get hyped when it really counts.

When visiting a ballpark in the US, it's not uncommon to observe fans who seem more focused on their food than the baseball game itself. These dedicated eaters can be seen constantly snacking, to the point where it becomes unclear if they're attending for love of the sport or the culinary delights. In fact, some fans go as far as leaving their seats entirely, opting to sit at a table in the concession stand. From there, they can enjoy their snacks while simultaneously watching the game on nearby TVs.

It may puzzle onlookers why these individuals choose to be at the ballpark if they're not going to watch the game from their assigned seats.

On the other hand, when attending a soccer game in the UK, one can't help but notice the gravity with which fans approach the sport. The atmosphere inside the stadium can be so focused and hushed that it resembles a library rather than a sporting event. Unlike in other countries, it is rare to see fans leaving their seats to use the restroom, except during halftime. If you dare to leave your seat during a crucial moment of the game, you may encounter disapproving looks from fellow fans. It's as if they view such actions as inconsiderate, interrupting the flow of the game. The level of engagement and concentration displayed by the fans is such that they rarely take a moment to indulge in food or snacks.

When you have the opportunity to attend a baseball game in Japan, one aspect that stands out is the extraordinary experience of the unified cheering in the outfield. While the atmosphere in the infield may be lively, it's the outfield that takes center stage. Almost all the spectators in that area don matching uniforms, creating a vibrant sea of colors. What makes it truly astounding is the synchronized coordination that takes place. With a simple cue from the cheerleader, the crowd engages in intricate moves and chants, displaying an impressive level of speed and precision that rivals even seasoned professional cheering squads.

As you can see, stadiums across the globe offer a range of pleasant experiences. But there's nothing quite like the baseball stadiums in South Korea. If you find yourself in the country between April and October, you absolutely must seize the chance to attend a game at one of their many stadiums scattered throughout the nation.

South Koreans' passion for baseball runs deep, making it the nation's most beloved sport. (I may be a baseball fan, but this is an unbiased opinion.) While soccer may have a higher participation rate, baseball holds the crown as the nation's favorite sport to watch. In the past, high school baseball captivated the nation's attention, but since the establishment of professional baseball in 1982, the sport has soared in popularity. The Korea Baseball Organization (KBO) oversees the league, which features 10 teams competing for the championship title, each representing a different region of the country. The level of baseball in South Korea is truly exceptional, highlighted by the remarkable achievements of its players. Their success is evident in the abundant accolades they have garnered, including Olympic gold medals. Furthermore, an impressive total of 26 talented individuals from South Korea have made their mark in the prestigious US Major League Baseball.

What makes Korean ballparks so special? Korean baseball fields are famous for their vibrant and unique atmosphere, primarily driven by the enthusiastic cheering culture. At the center of this culture are the spirited cheerleaders and their powerful amplifiers, which are cranked up to the maximum to ignite the crowd's energy. While there are regulations to lower the volume during crucial moments of the game, the stadiums are consistently filled with a constant buzz of excitement throughout the entire match. This fervor reaches its peak when the home team steps up to bat, presenting a golden opportunity to score.

Each team in Korean baseball features an extensive repertoire of chants and songs, comprising a diverse array of Korean hits, popular tunes, and even opera arias (with proper royalties duly paid). The lyrics are often tweaked to fit the occasion. But it doesn't stop at singing alone; fans exhibit their ingenuity through synchronized clapping and plastic stick-banging, each team adhering to its preferred rhythm. Leading the charge are the cheerleaders, who expertly orchestrate a blend of these diverse options, deftly adjusting the crowd's mood as the game progresses—whether it be at the beginning or end, with the team in the lead or trailing behind, and various other occasions.

In addition to cheering for the team, each player has their own dedicated entrance song or chant, which fills the stadium when they step onto the field, but only when the home team is playing. These songs are often based on famous existing melodies, ensuring that fans from different countries can recognize familiar tunes during their visit to the stadium. Along with the entrance song, each player also has a personalized chant with an upbeat rhythm. Die-hard fans are well-versed in all these melodies and lyrics, and they actively participate in the cheering with loud voices and enthusiastic movements. This dynamic atmosphere makes seats with a good view of the cheering section highly sought after, despite not providing the best view of the game or being the most expensive.

Korean baseball fans have ingeniously crafted a repertoire of chants and songs tailored to different game situations, contributing to the vibrant atmosphere of the sport. They have specific chants for when their team secures an impressive lead and another for before the bottom of the eighth inning, creating a heightened sense of anticipation. Additionally, they have celebratory songs that play when an opponent strikes out, as well as when their own player receives a walk. It's worth noting that there are separate chants designed for male and female spectators, often sung in alternating turns.

During the brief break between offense and defense, the cheerleaders in Korean baseball stadiums deliver an electrifying mini-performance that never fails to impress. They often showcase a hit song by a popular boy or girl group, setting the perfect mood for the crowd. And when the vibe is just right, fans eagerly take out their smartphones (or previously, lighters) and wave them in the air, creating a concert-like atmosphere with the lights twinkling throughout the stadium. As if that wasn't enough, the crowd even engages in a tradition known as the "Mexican wave," where everyone stands up and raises their hands in the air, producing a wave-like effect that ripples through the stadium. Although it is said to have originated from the 1986 World Cup in Mexico, Koreans use it way more than the Mexicans do.

Depending on the team, there are some other funky traditions that get thrown into the mix. Take, for instance, the bizarre practice of waving ripped-up newspapers in perfect unison, or inflating plastic bags until they're fit to burst and then wearing them like crazy hats. This is all part of the Lotte Giants' cheering culture, hailing from Busan - South Korea's second-biggest city. The plastic bag thing, in particular, took off like a rocket in 2005 and was a huge hit for a good long while. Unfortunately, it got the boot in 2021 as part of a push to cut down on single-use plastic. Get this: in the past, a whopping 1.5 million plastic bags were used for this cheer every year. (Yep, we're talking about garbage bags, folks. Cheering tools during the game, trash bags afterwards.) The Lotte Giants may not be top of the league, but their fans are known to be some of the most dedicated out there. They're famous for busting out their own specific dialect to boo the pitcher's pick-off throw, and when a foul ball is hit, they all scream in unison to give it to a nearby kid. If you're ever in Busan and there's a ball game happening, I say go check it out. Just be warned - if you don't speak Korean, you might struggle to keep up with the lingo.

Another well-loved tool for cheering in South Korean baseball games is a sketchbook. Fans keep a collection of different cheers and use the ones that fit the game situation. It's not noisy, doesn't involve any big gestures, and isn't a group activity, but it's still wildly favored. Why? Because of TV coverage, my friend. Professional baseball in South Korea has a whopping 720 regular season games each year, all broadcast live on TV and the internet. Of course, playoffs and the Korean Series are also broadcast live. By holding an open sketchbook, writing witty and humorous phrases, and displaying an eager expression, fans increase their chances of being captured by the cameramen who are constantly searching for captivating footage. At South Korean baseball stadiums, cracking jokes and showing off your wit are just as important as the sport itself.

You too can have a chance to appear on TV during a South Korean baseball game. All it takes is buying a jersey, putting it on, and using your body language to signal to someone wearing the same jersey who is engaged in sketchbook cheering that you'd like to give it a try. There's a high likelihood, over 90%, that they will gladly lend you their sketchbook, opening it to the right page. However, the probability of actually being featured on TV is lower. If you're determined to increase your chances, you can acquire more cheerleading gear, amplify your facial ex-

83

pressions and gestures, paint your face, don a red wig, or even unleash some eccentric dance moves. If you do happen to be captured on camera, you can always catch the replay online at any time. So why not give it a shot?

Another standout feature of Korean baseball stadiums is the impressive array of food options available to fans. In addition to the classic hot dogs and hamburgers, you'll discover a diverse selection of street food that might be unfamiliar to visitors but holds a special place in the hearts of locals. At Seoul's Jamsil Baseball Stadium, you can savor delectable pork belly lunch boxes, while in the coastal city of Busan, you can treat yourself to mouthwatering raw fish dishes. Some ballparks, such as Incheon SSG Landers Field and Changwon NC Park, even feature barbecue zones equipped with tables and grills, enabling fans to grill their own meats. Just remember to bring your own utensils and food—it's like camping at a baseball game! (While Korean baseball fans don't seem to eat as much as their American counterparts, they do eat a much wider variety of foods.)

Now, listen up folks, because I'm about to introduce you to the true MVP of ballpark food: chimaek. This enticing combination brings together Korean fried chicken and a cold beer (maekju), forming a culinary dream team. Fried chicken is no stranger to our taste buds, and beer is the most common alcoholic beverage in the world, yet surprisingly, there are few countries that enjoy eating both together. In fact, "chimack" is so beloved by Koreans that it's a must-try even if you don't go to the ballpark. Stay tuned for the next article, where we'll dive into the fascinating history behind this epic pairing.

Lastly, if you're wondering which team to root for at the ballpark, look no further than the Doosan Bears, the crème de la crème of the KBO (some may disagree - but this book is written by a devoted Doosan Bears fan). These guys were the original gangsters of professional baseball in South Korea and have been dominating the game for an impressive 42 years. They have an astonishing record of making it to the postseason 25 times and have clinched six championships, including the inaugural year of the KBO. And let's not forget their incredible seven-year streak of reaching the Korean Series from 2015 to 2021.

The team's relentless hustle on the field has earned them the nickname "Hustle Doo," and their unwavering determination has crowned them as "the most unwearied team." And let's not forget their proud moniker, "Miracle Doosan," which is a testament to their numerous incredible come-from-behind victories. With their stylish uniforms and captivating cheers, they truly are the complete package. You can catch them in action at Jamsil Baseball Stadium in Seoul, conveniently located near the Sports Complex subway station on lines 2 and 9.

# 6.

# Korea

# Fried Chicken and
# Chimaek

I confidently stated earlier that if you had only one meal in Korea, it should be samgyeopsal. Now, if you have the opportunity for two meals, my recommendation would be Chimaek. It was a tough decision, but after careful consideration, I believe the combination of crispy fried chicken and beer is a must-try experience in Korea. (Of course, there are many more Korean foods that will captivate your taste buds, so I encourage you not to limit yourself to just two meals and leave. I hope you'll stay a bit longer and indulge in at least ten meals or so.) Korean-style chicken is a delicious dish that perfectly complements a cold beer, but what exactly is it?

Chicken is a universally beloved food, and Koreans are no exception. In fact, they have been enjoying chicken for centuries, but historically, it was prepared through boiling. Actually, some of the classic Korean dishes that I'll suggest later also involve boiled chicken. However, it wasn't until the 1960s that Koreans began to consume chicken in a new way. A restaurant introduced rotisserie chicken to the public, and it quickly became a hit.

Rotisserie cooking wasn't a common practice in Korea, and using electricity to cook food was indeed a rarity back then. As a result, the dish was given a peculiar name - "electric grilled whole chicken." The restaurant that introduced this innovative cooking method, and continues to operate today, has a quirky name - Nutrition Center. During an era of poverty and limited food options, chicken served as a valuable source of protein for Koreans, making it a prized dish.

During the 1970s, a new trend emerged in Korea where the whole chicken was fried, and it quickly gained popularity. Some restaurants still offer this style of fried chicken today, preserving the original method. However, it wasn't until 1977 that the American-style of fried chicken, where the chicken is cut into pieces, battered, and then fried, made its debut in Korea. In 1984, the American brand KFC (Kentucky Fried Chicken) entered the Korean market, further fueling the widespread appeal of fried chicken. Since then, the fried chicken industry in Korea has experienced steady growth. Many fried chicken restaurants have competed with each other by adopting slightly different frying methods and flavors, and some have expanded their business by opening multiple franchise stores, thereby increasing their brand value.

However, two important events played a crucial role in the massive popularity of fried chicken culture in Korea: the 1997 foreign exchange crisis and the 2002 Korea-Japan World Cup.

After two decades of remarkable economic growth starting in the 1970s, South Korea faced a significant setback with the 1997 foreign exchange liquidity crisis, which also affected several other Asian countries. The South Korean government sought assistance from the International Monetary Fund (IMF) to navigate through the crisis, which had a profound impact on the Korean people for approximately four years. Even to this day, the term "IMF," though unfamiliar to most Koreans at the time, carries a sense of trauma for many. While acknowledging the

IMF's vital support during the crisis, the frequent use of phrases such as "IMF crisis" and "IMF debacle" has contributed to the negative association with the IMF. (Apologies to the IMF for any unintended implications.)

The 1997 financial crisis had a profound impact on the lives of Koreans, leaving a lasting impression and valuable lessons. The "Gold-collecting campaign" is still revered as a testament to the nation's resilience in the face of adversity. Around 3.51 million individuals contributed their stored gold, resulting in approximately 227 tons of gold being exported to address the foreign currency shortage. (In Korea, it is customary to gift a small gold ring on a child's first birthday, leading to many households having stored gold.) While the amount of gold collected and exported during the campaign accounted for only about one-tenth of the IMF loan, it played a crucial role in fostering a sense of national unity and collective determination to overcome the crisis. Although the gold export alone did not provide a definitive solution, the symbolic act of sacrificing precious possessions in the midst of economic hardship remains a powerful and cherished memory for many Koreans.

However, the impact of the financial crisis was far-reaching, leading to the bankruptcy of many companies, including large corporations, and forcing others to undertake extensive layoffs to avoid collapse. Widespread restructuring efforts were implemented, resulting in a sharp increase in unemployment. Overnight, countless individuals found themselves without jobs, receiving minimal severance and compensation.

As a result of the widespread unemployment caused by the 1997 crisis, many people in Korea, lacking specialized skills or capital, were forced to become self-employed. One accessible option was opening a franchise chicken restaurant, which had a relatively low barrier to entry. With the ingredients supplied by headquarters and the manual provided, anyone could learn how to fry chicken. In the 1990s, successful fried chicken companies began rapidly expanding their number of locations. This rise of Korean fried chicken is tied to the difficult circumstances that forced many Koreans to start their own businesses, in contrast to the origin of American fried chicken, which is rooted in the pain of black slaves.

Subsequently, "chicken" became synonymous with "fried chicken" to Koreans, rather than referring to the animal itself or other chicken-based dishes. To avoid confusion, I will use the term "chikin" to specifically describe Korean fried chicken from this point onwards. (Warning: It's not a typo.)

In 2002, South Korea had the honor of hosting the World Cup, coinciding with the growing prevalence of chikin. While baseball remains the most popular sport in the country, soccer also enjoys a robust following, especially when it comes to supporting the national team. South Koreans are just as passionate about the World Cup as any European nation. Despite being co-hosted with Japan, having the World Cup in their own country was a dream come true for many Koreans. The Korean team's remarkable performance captured the hearts of the nation as they won game after game and exceeded expectations by reaching the quarterfinals, surpassing their original goal of making it to the round of 16 by two stages.

During the World Cup, South Korea was swept up in a wave of excitement and celebration. On match days for the Korean team, large crowds of people adorned in red jerseys flocked to public squares throughout the country, with some gatherings attracting over a million enthusiastic fans. For those unable to join the lively street festivities, bars and movie theaters transformed into soccer viewing venues, replacing movies with live game broadcasts. Soccer matches could be seen on televisions everywhere, from train stations and hospitals to schools, workplaces, and homes.

Nobody knows the reason, but many of these spirited fans embraced 'chimaek' as if it were a precatory ritual, and the combination of chikin and beer became inseparable from the experience of watching soccer matches. The demand for chikin during the World Cup was so high that it was not uncommon for delivery services to have a waiting time of 2-3 hours to fulfill orders. (We will delve deeper into the extraordinary culture of efficient delivery services in Korea later.)

After the surge in popularity of chikin in the early 2000s, Korean fried chicken restaurants embarked on a journey of innovation, introducing a wide array of new recipes. In the past, there were only two main types of fried chicken: naked and marinated, with soy sauce marinated chicken being the exception. However, the landscape has drastically changed, and today, there is an overwhelming variety of chikin options, making it challenging to keep track. Korean chikin has become more diverse than Italian pizza, American hamburgers, or German sausages. Remarkably, there are now over 400 franchised chikin companies with multiple franchisees, alongside plentiful independently owned chikin restaurants. It is not uncommon to find even non-specialty pubs featuring chikin on their menu. Each chikin brand has at least ten different menu items, resulting in thousands of different types of chikin.

With some of the most famous brands boasting well over 1,000 stores in Korea alone, and over 2,000 when considering their international branches, it's natural to wonder about the total number of chikin restaurants in Korea. Prepare to be amazed. It is estimated that there are over 80,000 chikin restaurants in South Korea, surpassing the combined count of McDonald's (38,000) and Starbucks (34,000) worldwide. This staggering figure solidifies South Korea's status as a true "chikin republic."

One might assume that fried chicken is a simple and generic dish, lacking pronounced characteristics. However, this couldn't be further from the truth in South Korea. Many Koreans possess a remarkable ability to identify the specific brand of chikin they're eating with astonishing accuracy after just a single bite, and some can even discern it solely by its aroma. It is not uncommon for Koreans to have a particular favorite type of chikin, and there are enthusiasts who can proudly divulge the precise brand and menu item of a specific chikin after merely one taste. This ability is something that some Koreans take great pride in.

A few years ago, a delivery app company organized a whimsical event where individuals had the opportunity to take the "chimmelier exam" and earn a prestigious "chimmelier certificate." The term chimmelier cleverly combines the words chicken and sommelier. The exam consisted of both a written and practical section, with the latter challenging participants to identify and differentiate between various chikin brands in a blind taste test. Due to space limitations, only 500 lucky individuals were able to participate in the test, and the overwhelming demand led to a lottery system to select the fortunate participants.

How many people do you think would have applied? Over 570,000 enthusiastic individuals eagerly applied for the event. Among the applicants, a total of 27,000 people successfully passed the online test, setting the stage for the next phase. Through a fair lottery system, only 500 fortunate candidates were invited to partake in the offline test. Finally, a distinguished group of 47 individuals emerged victorious, earning the esteemed title of "chimmelier." Such was the event's widespread appeal that it was organized twice to accommodate the overwhelming demand, and there are a total of 166 chimmeliers through two events. However, it is important to note that due to protests by animal rights advocates at the test site, the event is no longer being held.

The Korean obsession with chikin not only showcases a culinary preference but also highlights some underlying social issues. Firstly, the proliferation of chikin restaurants reflects the disproportionately high rate of self-employment in South Korea. Despite a gradual decline, the country's self-employment rate remains around 25%, markedly surpassing the OECD average of 15.8%. Only Brazil, Chile, Colombia, Greece, Mexico, and Turkey have higher self-employment rates than South Korea.

One notable drawback of the South Korean economy lies in its insufficient availability of quality jobs relative to the size of the economy. Additionally, the labor market's inflexibility poses challenges in finding new employment once a job is lost. As a consequence, people's income levels tend to be unstable, and there is fierce competition among self-employed individuals, leading to financial losses or business closures for many of them. A vivid example of this can be seen in the character Song Kang-ho portrayed in the movie "Parasite," where he once opened a chikin restaurant that ultimately failed.

Moreover, the financial burden of launching and sustaining an independent business often contributes to mounting household debt. While the government is actively working to reduce the percentage of self-employed individuals, addressing this issue is complex and presents considerable challenges.

The second most pressing issue within the Korean chikin industry pertains to the conflicts between franchisees and the headquarters of franchised businesses. Given the diverse fees and marketing costs that the franchisor collects from the franchisee, in addition to the expenses for ingredients, the franchisee often struggles to make substantial profits, while the franchisor, on the other hand, benefits financially. This challenge is not exclusive to the chikin sector; it is a prevalent concern across various franchise industries, including 24-hour convenience stores.

Thirdly, a conflict arises between restaurants and delivery companies due to the highly developed delivery culture in Korea. Not only chikin and pizza, but also almost any type of food and goods can be delivered. This trend has seen a significant increase since the pandemic. With Statistics Korea reporting that in 2021, the average South Korean received 70.3 home delivery boxes per capita. Considering the economically active population alone, this figure amounts to 128.2 deliveries per capita. While specific data on the proportion of food delivery within these numbers is not available, the same statistics indicate that food delivery sales amount to $20 billion. Assuming an average meal cost of $10, we can estimate that approximately 2 billion meals are delivered in South Korea annually. With a population of 50 million people, this suggests that each person consumes an average of 40 meals per year through delivery services.

In the past, conflicts between restaurants and delivery companies were less common because restaurants handled deliveries through their own staff. However, with the rise of smartphone apps, food delivery orders have become heavily dependent on delivery platforms. This shift in the market has led to conflicts between smaller restaurants and the few dominant platforms, primarily centered around commission rates.

Fourthly, as the chikin market in South Korea has expanded and the market share of a few major companies has grown, concerns regarding unfair trade practices, such as price fixing, have emerged. Notably, the price of chikin sold by large franchise chains has been steadily increasing, with many menu items now exceeding $20. South Korea, being a relatively expensive country with some markets dominated by a few players, has seen instances of price gouging in diverse industries. However, when it comes to the price of chikin, Koreans are particularly sensitive. Perhaps, they may think chikin as a sort of "public good" due to their deep affection for this culinary delight.

As a traveler, it's indeed best to let Koreans handle the complexities of these issues while you enjoy the delicious chikin and a refreshing beer. Now, the question arises of where to go and what to order from the overwhelming number of chikin restaurants and menus. If you're looking for the most favored chikin brands, you can easily spot Kyochon, BBQ, and BHC, as they have nearly 5,000 branches across the country. Most of their signage is in English, with pictures showcasing their specialty dishes. Allow me to guide you on what to order. For Kyochon, I recommend trying the "ban-ban" original; for BBQ, the olive chicken "ban-ban"; and for BHC, the bburinkle combo. (Ban-ban means half-and-half, allowing you to taste two flavors in one order.) A single menu item from these brands is usually sufficient for two people. If you're still hungry, you can order additional dishes or explore other chikin restaurants which will surely be nearby.

It's worth noting that some chikin restaurants in Korea operate primarily as takeout or delivery establishments and may not have tables for dine-in customers. If you come across such a place, don't worry and simply look for another option that suits your preference. Alternatively, you can order your chikin to-go, which is a common practice among Koreans, and enjoy it at a nearby park or back at your accommodation. Here's a final tip: if you have limited time to explore Korean cuisine, consider having chikin as a late-night snack rather than for lunch or dinner. In fact, chikin is widely enjoyed as a choice for late-night dining among Koreans.

While chikin may not have originated in Korea and lacks a long-standing deep-rooted history, it has undeniably become a beloved national food. Once you've experienced the amazing flavors and deliciousness of Korean chikin, you might find yourself yearning to return to Korea just to indulge in its taste once more.

# 7.

# Kimchi,

# Doenjang,

# and ⬚Oldboy⬚

Among the trendy games enjoyed by young Koreans today is the "balance game." While the name might evoke thoughts of a physical workout, it is actually a fun and straightforward what-if game involving choices. In this game, players are presented with two options and must choose one. For example, they might be asked if they would rather receive $5 million right now but age 20 more years instantly, or staying as you are. Another question could be whether they would prefer to never brush their teeth for the rest of their life or never wash their hair.

The questions in the balance game can indeed be outrageous and extreme, to the point that some are too explicit to mention here. Others may contain risqué content that is better suited for adult participants. While the game may appear to be a lighthearted joke, it often leads people to genuinely ponder their choices and question, "why on earth do I have to choose between these absurd scenarios?"

In fact, the game was even posed to a presidential candidate on a TV show. During the show, he was asked if he would rather marry his current wife again or become president if he were born again. While the candidate may have intended to choose the latter option, he cleverly responded with "I don't think my wife would ever marry me again." Despite his clever response to a tricky question, the presidential candidate did not win the election. It remains unclear whether he would have gained more votes if he had chosen the former option. Now, let's turn the question to you: If you could only have one meal in Korea, which would you choose: Soju with pork belly or beer with chikin?

Asking most Koreans whether they'd rather give up kimchi jjigae or doenjang jjigae for the rest of their lives is equivalent to asking them to choose only one to live with among their children. Both dishes are so integral to Korean cuisine and culture that the mere thought of giving up one or the other is enough to elicit looks of shock, awe, and sheer horror. Kimchi jjigae and doenjang jjigae are more than just food - they're a part of Korean soul and identity.

The term "jjigae" translates to "stew" in English, but it encompasses more than just the meat in the dish—it also includes the flavorful broth. Now, let's delve into the details of kimchi and doenjang. We'll start with kimchi, a well-known and widely recognized fermented side dish. Perhaps you have had the pleasure of trying it before or at least heard about its popularity.

In the broadest sense, kimchi refers to a diverse range of fermented vegetable dishes prepared by salting and fermenting vegetables. The types and varieties of kimchi are extensive and often influenced by the main vegetable ingredient, additional ingredients used, level of fermentation, and even the shape of the dish. If you were to ask any Korean, they would likely be able to name a dozen different types of kimchi, and the total number of varieties can surpass several dozen when including lesser-known and unique types. Moreover, it's not uncommon for the same kind of kimchi to have multiple names.

In a more specific sense, kimchi specifically refers to a distinct

Korean dish that prominently features Napa cabbage as the main ingredient. It is seasoned with a blend of chili peppers, garlic, and salted fish, and undergoes a fermentation process before being consumed. It is worth noting that when you search for "kimchi" on Google, the most common result is "baechu (Napa cabbage) kimchi," which serves as the baseline type of kimchi.

Kimchi is not typically consumed as a standalone dish or as the main course. Instead, it serves as a crucial side dish that accompanies rice or other main dishes, and it is an essential ingredient in many Korean dishes. In reality, attempting to avoid kimchi during a visit to Korea, even for just a few days, is an almost impossible task. It's akin to embarking on a mission impossible, one that not even Tom Cruise could successfully accomplish.

Kimchi indeed has a rich and captivating history that spans over a millennium. However, one of the most pivotal moments in its history was the introduction of chili peppers, which is considered a momentous event. It is believed that chili peppers were introduced to the Korean peninsula in the late 16th or early 17th century. Prior to their arrival, kimchi did not possess its characteristic vibrant red color.

Certainly, I understand that delving into the vast world of kimchi can be overwhelming. The sheer variety and depth of the kimchi universe make it nearly impossible for anyone other than permanent residents of Korea to experience all its different types. Instead, I'm more than happy to share a couple more intriguing tidbits about kimchi with you.

Firstly, besides Napa cabbage, radish is another commonly used ingredient in kimchi. Kimchi made with diced large radishes is known as "kkakdugi" or cubed radish kimchi. It is one of the most commonly encountered types of kimchi in Korea and is often served at restaurants that specialize in dishes like samgyetang, gomtang, and seolleongtang, which we'll discuss in more detail later.

Secondly, there are certain types of kimchi that do not contain red pepper flakes and are known as "baek-kimchi" or white kimchi. White kimchi is made with Napa cabbage as the main ingredient and has a similar appearance to regular kimchi but without the red seasoning. In fact, it's the type of kimchi that has a longer history.

Thirdly, there is a type of kimchi called "mul-kimchi" or water kimchi. It is made with a clear liquid in which ingredients like

Napa cabbage and radish float. The broth of mul-kimchi can be transparent or slightly reddish in color, and it's important to not only consume the vegetables but also spoon the broth while eating it.

Fourthly, while some kimchi is consumed immediately after marination, most varieties require a period of aging. During this time, fermentation takes place, contributing to its signature flavor. The duration of the aging process depends on the storage temperature, usually ranging from one to two weeks. However, kimchi can be enjoyed for an extended period even after the fermentation is complete. When stored at the correct temperature, it can be consumed in small portions over several weeks or months, with the flavor evolving over time. In fact, some Koreans appreciate kimchi that has been aged for six months or longer, and there are even instances of carefully temperature-controlled aging for two to three years. While the increasingly sour taste may present a challenge to some foreigners, aged kimchi holds great value among Koreans. And no, they don't use the term "vintage" to describe it, although it may cost more.

Fifthly, it's quite common for Korean households to have a dedicated refrigerator specifically for storing kimchi. If you ever have the opportunity to explore a Korean home, don't be surprised to find two large refrigerators occupying valuable space in their usually compact living quarters. These kimchi fridges are approximately the same size as regular refrigerators but come with a higher price tag. To maintain the optimal condition of kimchi, the temperature in a kimchi fridge is set a few degrees lower than that of a standard fridge, typically around minus one degree Celsius (just below freezing). While kimchi takes center stage, it's not the sole occupant of these fridges. Koreans also utilize them to store various other items, ranging from meats and vegetables to beverages like beer. (The widespread use of kimchi fridges only became prevalent in the mid-1990s.)

As previously mentioned, kimchi is not just a simple side dish; it's also a vital ingredient in a variety of mouth-watering dishes. Take, for instance, kimchi jeon, a delectable kimchi pancake. To prepare this tasty treat, you mix shredded kimchi with flour and water, then fry it in a pan along with pork, clams, squid, or any other ingredients that tantalize your taste buds. Another enticing option is kimchi bokkumbap, which is kimchi fried rice. This dish involves stir-frying shredded kimchi with rice in a wok, creating a harmonious blend of flavors. For a hearty and flavorful meal, you can indulge in kimchi jjim, a braised kimchi dish. In this preparation, aged kimchi is simmered with pork or mackerel in a pot for an extended period, allowing the flavors to meld together. And let's not forget the heavenly combination of grilling kimchi alongside pork belly!

But, when it comes to the enchanting world of kimchi cuisine, few dishes can rival the savory and soul-warming goodness of kimchi jjigae. This stew holds such a special place in the hearts of Koreans that it's often considered the country's national dish. The key to a truly exceptional kimchi jjigae lies in the broth, which must possess a deep and rich flavor that can only be achieved by simmering kimchi with the perfect combination of ingredients. Commonly, this includes dried anchovies and pork, complemented by scallions, onions, and tofu to add an extra layer of deliciousness. But, there's no need to be boxed in by convention. You can experiment with different types of kimchi and other add-ins (like SPAM) to make your own unique flavor. This is precisely why every kimchi jjigae you encounter in restaurants across Korea offers a different taste.

Another captivating Korean comfort food to indulge in is doenjang jjigae. This delicious stew features a medley of vegetables, doenjang (soybean paste), and a flavorful broth, with doenjang taking center stage. If you find yourself curious about what exactly doenjang is and how it's made, you're not alone. Interestingly, while Koreans are familiar with doenjang, many are unaware of the intricate process involved in making it from scratch. In the past, it was a common practice for many Korean households to prepare doenjang at home. However, in modern times, the convenience of purchasing it from the supermarket has become the norm for most people.

To truly understand the art of making doenjang, we must explore the interconnected nature of three vital elements: doenjang (soybean paste), ganjang (soy sauce), and gochujang (red chili paste). These three components form an inseparable trio known as the "holy trinity" of Korean cooking. In Korean cuisine, "Jang" is a catch-all term for seasonings and condiments.

Alright folks, get ready to learn about the magical process of making Korean jangs! (Even Koreans are unfamiliar with it.) It all starts with some beans. To make doenjang, you begin by soaking and boiling the beans, then mashing and shaping them into cubes called "meju". After hanging the meju on twine to dry for a few weeks, they are moved to a warm place to ferment for an additional one to two weeks. Once the meju has sufficiently fermented, it is combined with a strong brine in a jar and left to sit for two to three months. Finally, the moist meju is delicately transferred into jars, resulting in the creation of doenjang.

To make soy sauce, the remaining liquid from the doenjang-making process is strained through a sieve to remove any scum, then boiled and allowed to cool down. Despite the seemingly straightforward recipe, don't be fooled by its simplicity. Achieving the right balance of flavors and textures requires precision and experience, especially since the process is highly susceptible to environmental factors like humidity and temperature. Even a slight deviation can result in a rotten or tasteless outcome. Now, where does gochujang fit into the picture?

To make gochujang, a portion of the dried meju is ground into a powder and combined with chili powder, salt, water, and grain flour such as rice or barley in precise ratios. The resulting gochujang can vary in spiciness, from mild to very hot, depending on the potency of the chili peppers used. (Naturally, even a less spicy gochujang might still taste spicy to you.) In summary, at the heart of doenjang, ganjang, and gochujang lies the same fundamental ingredient -- meju, a fermented soybean paste.

In the past, it was common to find several clay pots called 'jangdok' in the yard of traditional Korean households. These pots were used to store the homemade jangs, including doenjang, ganjang, and gochujang. The jangs would be carefully prepared and fermented, allowing them to last for a year or even longer. However, with the advent of modern convenience, many people now opt to store their jangs in plastic containers in the refrigerator.

In San Francisco, there's a prestigious establishment called Benu, which boasts an impressive three Michelin stars and consistently ranks among the world's best restaurants. As you approach the entrance, you can catch a glimpse of "meju" hanging in the air, while stacks of "jangdok" catch your eye on the side. These visual cues reflect the Korean-American Chef Corey Lee's strong culinary identity and his exceptional interpretation of Korean cuisine. I had the privilege of dining at Benu once, and it was truly an exceptional experience that ticked all the boxes. However, it's worth noting that the prices at Benu are quite high, which might be a deterrent for some. While the restaurant is undeniably fantastic, affordability could be a consideration for potential diners. (If this book turns out to be a success, I wouldn't mind indulging in another memorable meal at Benu.)

We've come a long way. Although the process of making doenjang can be challenging and intricate, crafting doenjang jjigae is a breeze if you have a good doenjang in your hand. This versatile dish embraces a range of vegetables like potatoes, zucchini, onions, carrots, and peppers, allowing for endless customization. The broth, typically prepared with dried anchovies or beef, yields a delightful umami flavor. While doenjang jjigae is classically not spicy, some prefer to add gochujang or red pepper flakes for a hint of heat. Tofu is a common addition, and seafood can further enhance the dish. The consistency of the broth can vary from thick and hearty to light and brothy, depending on the recipe. One thing is for sure, no two bowls of doenjang jjigae are the same, but they are always delicious and satisfying.

Rice, the beloved staple food of Koreans, is the perfect companion for doenjang jjigae or kimchi jjigae. While rice is commonly prepared as plain rice, it can also be a satisfying blend of various grains like barley, brown rice, soybeans, and red beans. Koreans do not consume rice at every meal, as Western-style meals with bread or various types of noodles are also popular. However, a typical Korean home-cooked meal includes rice, a variety of side dishes, and a steaming hot brothy dish like jjigae. While it is not uncommon to enjoy jjigae without rice, especially when indulging in pork belly, for the ultimate flavor experience, pairing your jjigae with a generous serving of rice is highly recommended. And if your doenjang jjigae happens to have a minimal amount of broth, fret not - simply mix it with rice and savor it like bibimbap.

While kimchi is a staple side dish and an essential ingredient in many Korean dishes, doenjang is not ordinarily used as a standalone ingredient. Instead, it is primarily utilized as a fundamental condiment that adds depth and complexity to a wide range of dishes. Additionally, doenjang serves as the base for other widely consumed condiments such as ssamjang, a savory sauce made by blending doenjang with garlic, gochujang, sesame oil, and other ingredients. Ssamjang is often paired with dishes like pork belly or raw fish, complementing their flavors and providing an enjoyable taste experience.

Gochujang, much like doenjang, is frequently utilized as a foundational ingredient for an array of dishes. While it can certainly be enjoyed on its own, such as a dip for vegetables or as a condiment alongside bibimbap, it is more commonly combined with other spices in varying ratios to create appetizing sauces or marinades for meats and vegetables. Gochujang's versatility shines through as it imparts a distinctive umami flavor to a multitude of Korean dishes, and its appeal is expanding globally as more individuals discover its inviting taste.

Attention, everyone! Let's delve into the fascinating world of soy sauce. You're probably familiar with soy sauce, as it's a common ingredient found in many cuisines, particularly in Japanese cuisine. However, it's important to note that Japanese soy sauce is produced using a different method from the one we discussed earlier. But fret not; we'll explore the intricate details of the differences between Korean soy sauce and Japanese soy sauce, as well as Korean doenjang and Japanese doenjang (miso) in the upcoming discussions. It's worth mentioning that Koreans have a deep appreciation for both types of soy sauce and doenjang.

You've surely come across the celebrated film "Oldboy," directed by Park Chan-wook. (If you haven't, you're missing out on one of the greatest masterpieces of Korean cinema.) In the movie, the protagonist, played by Choi Min-sik, endures 15 years of confinement with only fried dumplings to sustain him, all without knowing why he's there.. However, let's imagine for a moment if it had been kimchi jjigae or doenjang jjigae instead. Korean viewers might have been slightly less horrified, and the suspense of the film may have been slightly diminished. While no Korean would willingly choose to subsist solely on kimchi jjigae or doenjang jjigae for a lifetime, if they were to select one dish to consume for every meal for 15 years, it is highly probable that nine out of ten Koreans would opt for kimchi jjigae or doenjang jjigae. (I would be willing to wager that a greater number would ultimately choose kimchi jjigae after very careful deliberation.) These hearty bowls of stew represent the essence of Korean comfort food. Now, if you had to choose one dish to eat for 15 years, what would it be? More often than not, it would be your culture's soul food.

# 8.

# Uncovering the Hidden Gems of Korean History

Earlier, I mentioned that the Doosan Bears embody the spirit of "never give up, never surrender." This is not only due to their tenacity and determination on the field but also because their mascot is a bear, which symbolizes unwavering persistence in Korean culture.

Bears indeed hold a significant place in wide-ranging aspects of human culture. They have a rich history in mythology, art, literature, and folklore, with their presence spanning across a diversity of cultures throughout the world. In some cases, cities have been named after bears, such as Berlin in Germany and Bern in Switzerland, reflecting the enduring symbolism associated with these majestic creatures. Bears have even been immortalized in the night sky, with constellations named after them, further emphasizing their prominence in human imagination. Moreover, bears have found their way into the hearts of people through beloved characters like Winnie the Pooh and teddy bears, becoming symbols of warmth, comfort, and strength.

Despite the popularity of bears in diverse cultures, Korea appears to be unique in its use of bears as a symbol of perseverance. Even in Anglo-American cultures where the word "bear" has the meaning of "endure", bears are often associated with traits such as fierceness, dedication, or cuteness, rather than patience.

Every Korean is familiar with the foundational myth of their country, which has several variations, but the most representative one goes as follows: In ancient times, Hwanung, the son of Hwanin, the Lord of Heaven, descended from the heavens along with 3,000 followers and established a city at the foot of Mount Paektu. A bear and a tiger approached him, expressing their desire to become human. Hwanung agreed to grant their wish under the condition that they stayed in a cave for 100 days, consuming only garlic and mugwort while avoiding sunlight. The tiger gave up halfway through, but the bear persevered and transformed into a woman named Ungnyeo. Eventually, Ungnyeo and Hwanung's son, Dangun, went on to establish Gojoseon (Old Joseon) on October 3, 2333 B.C., a date still celebrated as a national holiday in Korea, despite the lack of historical evidence supporting Dangun's founding of the nation on that particular day.

According to Korea's founding myth, there is a belief that all Koreans are descended from bears, symbolizing the virtue of patience. Bears are known for their endurance and ability to survive in a cave for 100 days with a limited diet of mugwort and garlic. Additionally, there is a humorous reference to Koreans being able to survive solely on fried dumplings for 15 years, highlighting their perceived patience. However, despite the mythological association with patience, modern-day Koreans are often perceived as being constantly in a rush. This raises the question of why this phenomenon exists. Is it because Koreans are an unprecedented people who are usually in a hurry but also exhibit exceptional patience during times of crisis?

Now, I don't want to burst anyone's bubble, but let's face it: myths are just myths. And it's highly unlikely that a nation with a fully-formed government actually existed way back in

2333 BC. We can be pretty sure that Gojoseon did exist at some point, and that it hung around for a while before finally falling apart around 108 BC. But when exactly it became a state, or where its capital was located, are still up for debate. Nevertheless, South Koreans are taught in school that their nation has been around for an impressive 5,000 years.

After the fall of Gojoseon, the Three Kingdoms era emerged, with Goguryeo, Baekje, and Silla vying for control of the Korean Peninsula and parts of Northeastern China for centuries. Among them, Silla eventually rose as the dominant power and established the Unified Silla period. While the state of Silla claimed a thousand-year duration, historians estimate its actual reign to be around 6-7 centuries. Nonetheless, it left a profound impact as a vibrant center of Buddhist culture. Following the Unified Silla, a brief period of three separate states ensued before the rise of the Goryeo and Joseon dynasties. Goryeo thrived for nearly 500 years, from 918 to 1392, while Joseon endured for over 500 years, from 1392 to 1910. Although this historical account may seem a bit tedious, fear not, for we are about to conclude the less eventful part. So kindly "bear" with us for just a little longer.

From 1910 to 1945, Korea was under Japanese colonial rule.

After gaining independence in 1945, the country was split into North and South Korea, leading to a period of unrest. The two Koreas formed separate governments in 1948 and engaged in the Korean War from 1950 to 1953. At the end of the war, both Koreas were left impoverished, but over the past 70 years, while South Korea has evolved into the prosperous and modern nation you're familiar with, its northern counterpart has taken a vastly different path, becoming the country you also know well, but with a very different trajectory.

To sum it up, the last 2,000 years of Korean history can be traced through the Three Kingdoms (Goguryeo, Baekje, and Silla), Unified Silla, Goryeo, Joseon, and the Republic of Korea. Unless you're studying for the Korean citizenship exam, there's no need to get into the nitty-gritty details. But understanding some historical context can make your visit to Korea much more captivating.

Well, let's get started with the name. "Korea" as we know it today got its name from the Goryeo dynasty. It was at this point in history that the world started to take notice of Korea. The next dynasty to come around was Joseon(or Chosun), which, fun fact, was the same name of a BC-era country. To differentiate it, old one is called "Gojoseon," which translates to "Old Joseon." Joseon dynasty lasted over 500 years until the early 1900s.

Although commonly referred to as South Korea and North Korea, the official names of the two countries are quite different from what we know. The Republic of Korea is the official name for South Korea and the Democratic People's Republic of Korea is the official name for North Korea. Interestingly, both countries still include "Korea" in their English names. However, the official "Korean" names are completely different from each other, and do not have "Korea" or "Goryeo" either. South Korea's name includes the word "Daehan," while North Korea's name includes the word "Joseon."

Before the end of the Joseon Dynasty in 1910, the country underwent a name change in 1897, when the king declared an "empire" and began referring to himself as emperor. The word used for the new name was "Daehan". A few decades later, after the country's division, South Korea chose a new name, while North Korea chose to retain a dynastic name that dated back 500 years. Some might even say it's fitting for North Korea, which resembles a "Kim" Dynasty. (North Korean leader Kim Jong Un, whose name you've probably heard, is the grandson of Kim Il

Sung, the founder of North Korea, and the son of the previous leader, Kim Jong Il.)

It's noteworthy to note that some of the names of the ancient kingdoms that existed on the Korean Peninsula still have a lasting impact today. Silla (or shilla) is a name commonly used for hotel and university, while Goryeo (or Goryo) is used for university, steel company, and pharmaceutical company. Joseon (or Chosun) is a favored name for newspaper, hotel, and university, and Daehan is widely used by airline, insurance company, logistics company, theater, and flour company. It is much more common to find the names of these historical Korean kingdoms in the names of small businesses and restaurants rather than larger corporations. Silla, Goryeo, Joseon, and Daehan are celebrated choices for business names in Korea. It's notable that one university writes its name in English as "Korea University," but in Korean as "Goryeo University."

Secondly, it is worth noting that despite its long history, South Korea has never been a feudal state like medieval Europe. Rather, it has always been a centralized state with a strong monarchy. While there have been periods when the royal power was particularly strong or weak, even during the weaker periods, power was shared by high-ranking officials in the central government, not local warlords seeking to expand their own power. Though some local officials may have abused their power, they were merely agents of the king and corrupt officials, and there were plenty of checks and balances in place. This absence of local warlords seeking power has contributed to the lack of civil war in Korean history, with only a few small-scale rebellions. Moreover, the high level of cultural and artistic development during all periods can also be attributed to the strong central government and minority ruling class. These historical facts may help explain the large population in Seoul and the pronounced gap between Seoul and the rest of the country. Like a well-known proverb in Korea states, "If it's a horse, send it to Jeju island; if it's a man, send it to Seoul."

Throughout its history, Korea has experienced several devastating wars due to foreign invasions. In the 13th century, the war with the Mongol Empire lasted for decades, and while Korea was not conquered, it was forced to pay tribute to the Mongols for a period of time. In the 16th century, the war with Japan lasted for seven years and caused great destruction to Korea. Despite winning against Japan, Korea suffered tremendous losses. The Korean hero General Yi Sun-shin, who led the victory against Japan, is still one of the most revered figures in Korea. On the other hand, Korea has not engaged in any acts of invading other countries. While some suggest this may be due to the country's lack of power to expand its territory, textbooks often attribute it to the Korean people's peaceful and gentle nature.

Thirdly, Korea didn't exactly get with the times when it comes to modernization. They never had a dramatic citizen revolution to overthrow their monarchy and turn into a republic, and they were pretty much cut off from the rest of the world during the 18th and 19th centuries thanks to a "closed-door policy". As a result, the adoption of modern technologies and institutions was slower compared to other nations. In the early 20th century, just as Korea was beginning to catch up, Japan colonized the country. Although there were attempts at modernization during this period, they were primarily driven by Japan's control over Korea and were not always beneficial for the Korean people.

In the aftermath of decolonization, the subsequent seven decades in Korea were akin to a thrilling rollercoaster ride. A nation with a history spanning over a millennium was torn apart and engulfed in a grueling three-year war. However, the resilient people fought back against dictatorship and established a flourishing democracy, while simultaneously propelling their economy forward through a fervor for world-class education and unwavering dedication. Their achievements surpassed mere prosperity, as they also became a "cutting-edge" country, partly due to the global phenomenon of K-pop. South Korea managed to condense numerous milestones, generally requiring other nations 100 or 200 years, into a phenomenal span of just 50 years.

Here's an example that highlights the incredible economic growth of South Korea: After the devastation of the Korean War, General MacArthur, then commander-in-chief of the Allied forces, famously predicted that it would take at least 100 years to rebuild Korea. The situation was so dire that several countries, including the United States, provided aid to South Korea, amounting to an estimated $60 billion over the decades. At one point, foreign aid accounted for a quarter of the country's budget.

However, since the 1990s, South Korea has experienced a remarkable reversal of fortune, transforming into a generous provider of aid to other nations. It is the only country in the world to have transitioned from being an aid recipient to becoming an aid donor. In 2021, South Korea provided a staggering $2.86 billion in foreign aid, ranking 15th among the 29 members of the OECD's Development Assistance Committee (DAC). Despite this achievement, South Korea's aid-to-GNI ratio of 0.16% is less than half the average for DAC members. Consequently, the South Korean government and many of its citizens are advocating for increased aid contributions in the future.

Fourthly, the relationship between South Korea and China holds an intriguing place historically. China, a major global player today, had an even greater influence in Asia in the past. South Korea was deeply influenced by Chinese culture, adopting elements such as Chinese characters, and many intellectuals embraced the idea that "China is the center of the world." While Korea was never a Chinese colony, it lived under Chinese influence for an extended period, akin to a poor younger brother under the authority of a powerful older brother.

During the 16th century Japanese invasion of Korea, China sent troops to aid Korea, and tragically, up to 30,000 Chinese soldiers lost their lives. For the following 200 years, Korea regularly dispatched special envoys to China as a form of tribute, while Chinese envoys were warmly received and treated with utmost hospitality. However, when Japan emerged victorious in its war against China in the late 19th century and subsequently annexed Korea in the early 20th century, both China and Korea shared a sense of empathy and solidarity, as the saying goes, "misery loves company."

The mid-20th century and beyond brought even greater complexity to the relationship between South Korea and China. The Korean War, initiated by a surprise attack from North Korea, initially saw the North making striking advances and nearly achieving a swift victory. However, the intervention of UN forces, including the United States, shifted the balance and brought the South to the verge of success. Subsequently, China entered the war, leading to a prolonged stalemate that resulted in the country being divided as it was before the conflict.

In the years that followed, while South Korea experienced rapid development, China's progress was comparatively slower, leading to a certain degree of dismissiveness among some Koreans towards China and its people. However, as a country heavily reliant on exports, South Korea has become increasingly dependent on China's thriving economy, which has become a force that cannot be ignored. Given China's growing influence and the recurring nuclear tests conducted by North Korea, South Korea often finds itself having to gauge China's stance and disposition.

South Korea finds itself in a difficult position as it seeks to maintain good economic relations with China while also grappling with conflicting emotions regarding Chinese investment to Korean real estates and job opportunities in Korea. However, the most significant factor in the worsening of Sino-South Korean relations has been China's distortion of history. China's claims that Goguryeo, one of the three ancient Korean kingdoms, was part of China, as well as its assertion that kimchi and "hanbok" (traditional Korean costume) have Chinese origins, have been met with strong opposition and have fueled anti-Chinese sentiment in Korea. (These claims are as far-fetched as Spain claiming to be the originator of pizza or Germany asserting to be the birthplace of champagne.)

Furthermore, China's disregard for intellectual property rights has caused additional strain on Sino-South Korean relations. Unauthorized production of knockoffs of famous Korean products and unlicensed distribution of Korean TV shows have been common occurrences. In addition, the Chinese government has banned Korean dramas from airing in China and Korean singers from performing in China. Moreover, the COVID-19 pandemic has contributed to the rise of anti-China sentiment in South Korea. According to a 2022 survey by the Pew Research Center in the U.S., South Koreans' unfavorable perception of China reached a staggering 80%, a stark contrast from just 31% in 2002. While anti-China sentiment has risen in many other countries since the pandemic, South Korea stands out as a notable exception.

Fifthly, let's delve into the relationship between Korea and Japan. These two countries have had a long history of interaction, which is not surprising given their close proximity. Korea is located at the northeastern end of the Eurasian continent, while Japan is situated just across the water, with the Pacific Ocean to the east. Throughout ancient times, multifarious cultures and people have migrated from Korea to Japan, resulting in cultural influences. In fact, historical records even suggest that the current king of Japan is a descendant of the royal family of Baekje, one of the three ancient Korean kingdoms. This fact was confirmed by the king of Japan himself in 2001.

During the medieval period, Korea and Japan had a complicated relationship that was neither fully friendly nor hostile.

However, Japan proved to be a thorn in Korea's side for many centuries, as Japanese pirates frequently raided Korean coasts starting in the 13th century. It wasn't until the 16th century that Korea-Japan relations took a definitive turn for the worse when Japan launched an invasion of Korea and engaged in a brutal seven-year war that caused immense suffering for the Korean people. Fast forward to the late 19th and early 20th centuries, Japan eventually annexed Korea, showcasing its modernization while Korea struggled to keep pace.

During the 35-year colonization period from 1910 to 1945, the Korean people experienced immense suffering and hardships. Countless innocent civilians were subjected to torture, imprisonment, and executions by the Japanese colonial authorities. Furthermore, the Japanese exploited Korea's valuable natural resources, confiscating grains and underground resources for their own benefit. Additionally, Koreans were forced to relinquish their Korean names and adopt Japanese names, and the teaching of the Korean language was prohibited. Many Koreans were forcibly taken to Japan as laborers, and during World War II, a myriad of women were coerced into becoming "comfort women" for the Japanese military.

In the almost 80 years since the end of colonization, significant changes have occurred in the relationship between Korea and Japan. Both countries have emerged as major players in the global economy, fostering extensive exchange and collaboration across myriad fields. There is a strong mutual fascination with each other's cuisine and culture, and both countries have become beloved destinations for tourists from the other. However, the deep wounds inflicted during the 16th century's Imjin War and the 35 years of colonization continue to affect their relationship, and many Koreans still perceive Japan as a rival that needs to be surpassed. A soccer match between these two nations often carries intense emotions, as Korean players and fans consider it unacceptable to lose to Japan. Moreover, there are two sensitive issues that contribute to Koreans' negative view of Japan: the problem of comfort women and the territorial dispute over Dokdo, a small group of islets.

During World War II, Japan committed grave atrocities across Asia, including the abduction and enslavement of women as sex slaves in military brothels. The United Nations estimates that approximately 210,000 women were affected, with around 70% of them being Korean (although Japan claims it was only around

50,000). These women, often referred to as "comfort women," endured unimaginable suffering, and their harrowing experiences continue to haunt them to this day. Sadly, the Japanese government has not fully acknowledged its responsibility for these crimes. It has also not provided adequate compensation or sincere apologies to the victims. This lack of accountability has deeply disappointed many Koreans, who draw comparisons to Germany's genuine efforts to confront its dark past, such as acknowledging the Holocaust and bringing war criminals to justice.

Dokdo may be small, but it holds immense importance for Koreans. This tiny island, located off the eastern tip of the country and measuring less than 0.2 square kilometers, has been recognized as Korean territory for centuries. Numerous historical records and ancient maps confirm its Korean heritage, and it is currently inhabited by around 50 Koreans. Despite this, Japan has been making its own territorial claims, and in recent years, the dispute has only intensified, with Dokdo even being included in Japanese school textbooks as Japanese territory. For Koreans, Dokdo represents more than just a piece of land—it is a symbol of sovereignty.

Koreans indeed hold a deep attachment to Dokdo. Many South Koreans are familiar with the precise coordinates of Dokdo (132 degrees East longitude, 37 degrees North latitude) and possess knowledge about its climate, size, number of wells, and the marine life in its surrounding waters. Some can even cite the exact title, page, and line of the specific book where the owner-ship of Dokdo by Korea is mentioned. Surprisingly, this is not a joke or exaggeration. It is attributed to a well-known song titled "Dokdo is Our Land," which was released in the 1980s and remains popular today. The song's lyrics contain the aforemen-tioned information, and interestingly, the melody of its first part shares similarities with the famous "Jessica Jingle" from the mov-ie Parasite. (Can you remember? Jessica, Only child, Illinois, Chicago, and Classmate Kim Jin-mo, He's your cousin.) Believe it or not, this catchy melody has become a mnemonic tool for many Koreans to memorize various facts. It's an effective and fun way to retain information. Why not give it a try yourself?

If you ever find yourself in South Korea, remember one word: "Dokdo." Why, you may ask? Well, uttering "Dokdo is Korean Territory" at a restaurant might surprise you with some free food. And if you happen to be in a difficult situation and need assistance, starting with this magic word might improve your chances of getting some help from the locals.

9.

# Why are Koreans #1 in these particular metrics?

_____

You can't deny that genetics plays a part in shaping an ethnic group's customs and habits. But let's not forget the shared experiences of a people over many generations. The ups and downs of the last century have definitely left their mark on Koreans, shaping their unique folkways.

For centuries, from ancient times until the late 1800s, Koreans followed a Confucian tradition that placed a great emphasis on loyalty. Despite being a non-affluent nation, it remained stable with a richly individual language and culture. While the majority of commoners who did not belong to the gentry class("yangban") led difficult lives due to the caste system, they were somewhat resigned to their fate. The country was agrarian, and there was a strong sense of community among the people. The political system, represented by the king, was accepted (to a certain extent) as working for the benefit and happiness of the people.

In the late 19th century, turbulent times began, and in the early 20th century, the country was colonized. The people, who did nothing wrong, suffered greatly because of their incompetent leaders. After a dogged resistance, the country was eventually reclaimed, but it was followed by division and war. The people's faith in the government was shattered, and they were faced with destruction, chaos, and poverty. As a result, they realized that they could not rely on anyone else or any other country for their protection and survival, leading to a focus on practicality over idealism. "In the modern world, knowledge is power, which is why education is so important. If you don't empower yourself, you're powerless." This idea was prevalent on a personal level, and on a national level as well.

Two keywords that have emerged in Korean culture are "gakjadoseng" and "gukppong". "Gakjadoseng" means "finding one's own way to survive", reflecting a sense of individualism and competition that has replaced the conventional emphasis on community and collective identity. This phrase also carries a sense of melancholy or weariness, suggesting that navigating life independently can be challenging and burdensome. "Gukppong", on the other hand, combines the words for "country" and "methamphetamine" and signifies extreme and irrational patriotism. While patriotism has long been an important value in Korean society, "gukppong" carries a negative connotation.

Fortunately, the culture of self-reliance that prevailed in Korean society for a long time is gradually diminishing. With the country's increasing wealth, the once weak welfare system has significantly improved, leading to a more relaxed society and the emergence of a culture that values caring for the socially disadvantaged. People have come to realize that their own happiness is more important than competing with others, and they are paying more attention to values like distribution and equity, which were often overlooked in the past in favor of purely quantitative growth. (Although the culture of self-reliance is becoming less pervasive, it still exists to a notable extent in Korean society.)

The term gukppong has gained widespread use in the past decade to describe a specific kind of patriotism particular to

Koreans. Korea is one of the few countries to have maintained its language and culture for over a thousand years with minimal ethnic mixing and few border changes. During times of national crisis, such as war, Koreans have come together to form armies and resist foreign powers. While Koreans may openly acknowledge their government's incompetence or criticize certain customs, they tend to react negatively when such criticisms come from outsiders. This attitude is reflected in the saying, "I can criticize my own country, but I cannot tolerate foreigners doing the same."

Koreans have a strong concern in how they are perceived by foreigners. Furthermore, they place a lot of importance on so-called "global standards" and are overly obsessed with numbers like "OECD average". This is probably due to the painful result of living in isolation for hundreds of years without foreign interaction until the end of the 19th century, like a 'babe in the woods.' Moreover, this desire may stem from the stunning progress they have achieved in recent decades. In other words, they want to objectively measure how far they have come. It's like a student who has studied very hard and is waiting for the next exam.

The tendency for Koreans to seek validation from foreigners is often manifested in their eagerness to ask the question, "Do you know OOO?" without providing any context. Common examples of "OOO" include PSY, Gangnam Style, Kim Yuna, and kimchi. More recently, "Parasite" and "Squid Game" have also been added to the list. (However, BTS is an exception to this rule, as Koreans assume that everyone already knows them.) When a foreigner responds positively, Koreans feel pleased, and if the foreigner expresses admiration for the mentioned item, Koreans become even more thrilled. It's important to note that this question is not limited to everyday interactions with foreigners on the street; even reporters interviewing foreign celebrities in front of TV cameras have been known to ask this question, although it is generally considered impolite.

Actually, this book has the potential to spark a controversy surrounding "gukppong." Some individuals who are wary of extreme patriotism might criticize my positive depictions of Korea, while those who strongly embrace it may criticize my negative portrayals. (However, I have made a conscious effort to maintain an objective perspective throughout the book.)

In any case, Koreans have a strong inclination towards monitoring their country's rankings across multiple categories. They strive to achieve higher rankings in areas where they excel and work diligently to improve in areas where they fall behind. Let's take a look at some of these rankings to help you understand how unique South Korea's culture is.

First, Korea boasts one of the world's lowest illiteracy rates and one of the highest university enrollment rates. The country's own language and script, known as Hangeul, which we'll examine further later, makes it remarkably easy for its citizens to read and write. It's safe to say that very few Koreans cannot read Hangeul, with a basic illiteracy rate that's nearly zero. Furthermore, South Korea's university enrollment rate stands at an impressive 70%, a figure significantly exceeding the OECD average of roughly 40%. As previously mentioned, Koreans historically staked their lives on their children's education as a means to escape poverty. The wage gap between college graduates and those without higher education was substantial, although it's gradually narrowing over time.

But let's not jump to conclusions about Korea's literacy rate just yet. While the ability to read and write may be widespread, there are concerns about functional literacy and critical thinking skills. According to the OECD's International Adult Literacy Surveys (IALS), which assess prose literacy, document literacy, and quantitative literacy, Korea ranks in the lower middle range in all three categories. Furthermore, when the survey focuses solely on university graduates, the results are even more disappointing. This could be attributed to the high rate of university enrollment, which might contribute to a lower overall average level of competency.

One possible explanation for these results is the education system in Korea, which has been criticized for its emphasis on rote learning and memorization rather than fostering critical thinking and practical skills. Another contributing factor could be the lack of a strong reading culture in the country. (It's a well-known fact that Koreans aren't big readers. Even books with a good reputation, like some I've written in the past, don't seem to fly off the shelves in Korea. That's why I decided to write a book aimed at foreigners instead.) Furthermore, the issue of an oversupply of college graduates exacerbates the problem by creating an imbalance in the job market. White-collar jobs are scarce. Blue-collar jobs, on the other hand, are more abundant. This creates difficulties for university graduates seeking suitable employment opportunities.

Secondly, Korea stands as a global leader in several industries that have been pivotal to its spectacular economic growth. To begin with, as a powerhouse in the realm of information technology, Korea takes the lead in internet speeds and smartphone adoption worldwide. Depending on the source and time of day, Korea's internet speeds are three to four times faster than the global average. Smartphone usage stands at around 95%, and the nation ranks among the most advanced globally in the commercialization of 5G technology.

Its online gaming industry is also very advanced, and its e-sports scene, where professional gamers compete, is among the best in the world. Moreover, it excels in memory semiconductors, commanding a substantial 70% combined market share through industry giants like Samsung Electronics and SK Hynix. The country's shipbuilding industry is also highly developed, dominating the global market with over 40% of the world's ships being constructed in Korea.

Korea's steel industry, while not the largest by market share, hosts the world's largest and second-largest steel mills. Additionally, the content industry, which you may be familiar with, is another arena where Korea has made noteworthy strides in recent years. The nation's influence in movies, dramas, pop music, and more is clearly evident.

Thirdly, Korea presents an compelling case when it comes to carbon neutrality, showcasing both positive and negative indicators. On the positive side, Korea is on par with Germany in having the world's best waste separation system. This accomplishment can be attributed, in part, to the long-standing policy of using government-mandated and expensive garbage bags for non-recyclable waste. However, despite this success, Koreans still generate a considerable amount of plastic waste. In fact, the country ranks as the world's third-largest producer of plastic waste per capita (88kg), trailing behind only the United States (130kg) and the United Kingdom (99kg). This situation may be partly attributed to the absence of a cost associated with discarding recyclable waste. Additionally, a particularly developed delivery culture in Korea may also play a role.

Furthermore, Koreans are heavy users of electricity, ranking third in per capita electricity consumption among 34 OECD countries, surpassed only by Canada and the United States. As a result, Korea stands among the top 10 countries worldwide in terms of total carbon emissions, and its per capita emissions are more than double the global average. Although efforts are being made, achieving carbon neutrality in Korea remains a challenging goal due to several factors, including the country's export-oriented industrial structure.

Fourthly, Koreans work the longest hours in the world. According to the OECD, as of 2020, Koreans worked an average of 1,908 hours per year. Although this is significantly lower than in the past, it still ranks third globally, following Mexico (2,124 hours) and Costa Rica (1,913 hours). It is also 221 hours longer than the OECD average of 1,687 hours, meaning that Koreans work nearly an extra hour every day compared to workers in other OECD countries. Despite various factors like the percentage of part-time workers and self-employed individuals, it is evident that Koreans work longer hours compared to the United States and developed European countries. The long working hours are further exacerbated by the fact that Koreans also have the longest average commuting time of 58 minutes, compared to the OECD average of 28 minutes. Due to long working hours and extended commutes, there is little time for rest or leisure activities.

By the way, regrettably, labor productivity in Korea remains among the lowest in the OECD countries. Some attribute this to workers being less efficient due to their long work hours, which could be a possible explanation. It is noteworthy that most Korean workers take a solid one-hour lunch break, and it is commonly accepted to return to work a little over an hour later, as it is not uncommon for people to work past their official end of the work day. (But they don't take naps.) However, there is another crucial factor to consider. Labor productivity does not solely measure the quantity of goods a worker produces but rather the value added by the worker in terms of money, which is strongly related to the worker's wage level. If a worker earns twice as much for the same work, their productivity is measured as twice as high. Higher average wages in a country are typically associated with higher productivity rates, and Korea's high percentage of self-employed and service workers, whose average wages are low, contribute to the country's low labor productivity rate.

Fifthly, Korea's rankings in gender equality indices are disheartening. The country's position on the Gender Gap Index (GGI) from the World Economic Forum is 99th out of 146 countries, indicating significant gender disparities. Similarly, on the United Nations Development Program's (UNDP) Gender Development Index (GDI), Korea ranks 57th out of 62 countries. Additionally, Korea holds the lowest rank on The Economist's Glass-ceiling Index. Although the UNDP's Gender Inequality Index (GII) places Korea 11th out of 189 countries, it is important to note that this index heavily relies on healthcare and education infrastructure and may not adequately reflect gender discrimination. It may be fair to say that Korea is not a very good place to be a woman. Meanwhile, factors such as a patriarchal culture, laws related to sexual crimes and stalking, and the gender-specific military service further contribute to gender conflicts, particularly among the younger generation.

In addition to gender inequality, South Korea also grapples with a serious wealth disparity issue. The relative poverty rate, which indicates the percentage of households earning 50% or less of the median income, stands at 15%, making it the second highest among OECD countries, surpassed only by the United States. The situation is further exacerbated for the elderly population, as they experience an even higher poverty rate, compounding the social and economic challenges faced by the country.

Sixthly, South Korea is confronted with one of the world's lowest fertility rates and one of the highest rates of aging. The issue of low birth rates is particularly critical. Currently, Korea has the lowest fertility rate globally, with a total fertility rate (TFR) of only 0.78 in 2022. To provide a comparison, Japan, which also grapples with a persistent low birthrate, has a TFR of 1.26 in 2022. Korea implemented birth control policies in the past to curb population growth. Following the baby boom after the Korean War in the 1950s, the fertility rate exceeded 6.0. However, from the early 1960s to the early 1980s, stringent birth control measures were enforced, leading to a fertility rate below the replacement level of 2.1 by 1983. The decline has continued since then. Various factors have contributed to this decline, including the 1997 foreign exchange crisis, the 2009 global financial crisis, and the increasing participation of women in the workforce. However, the primary challenge lies in Korea being regarded as a "challenging country for parenting." Despite the government's efforts to promote childbirth starting in 2003, the fertility rate has steadily decreased, reaching 0.98 in 2018, marking the first time Korea had a fertility rate below 1.0 in the world. Over the course of the following four years, the rate further declined to

0.78, raising concerns about the prospect of "national extinction".

Korea is grappling with a concerning rate of population aging, stemming from a combination of low fertility and increasing life expectancy. Currently, 17.5% of the population is aged 65 or older, which may not appear alarming when compared to other nations. However, the underlying trend is worrisome. If this trend persists, Korea is projected to transition into an ultra-elderly society by 2025, with over 20% of the population aged 65 or older. Furthermore, by 2045, this proportion is anticipated to rise to 37%, establishing Korea as the world's oldest country.

Seventhly, on the other end of the spectrum from 'gukppong' is the term 'Hell-Joseon,' which depicts a perception that present-day Korean society is excessively challenging to live in. The addition of "hell" to the name of the Joseon Dynasty, a historical period in Korea, reflects a sense of self-mockery and discontent with the current state of the country. This sentiment arises from various factors, including long working hours, intense competition, a significant wealth gap, outrageously high real estate prices, and a shortage of desirable employment opportunities. Consequently, Korea faces one of the highest suicide rates globally, with 24.6 suicides per 100,000 people annually, more than double the OECD average.

Indeed, the term "Hell-Joseon" is predominantly used by young individuals who are yet to establish a solid footing in society. Given the prevailing economic circumstances, a multitude of predictions suggest that the current generation of young Koreans could be the first in history to experience a lower standard of living compared to their parents. Compounding their concerns, they also face the burden of supporting the older generations who were born during the baby boom era. As individuals of childbearing age contemplate the future, they express apprehension about the notion of bringing a child into a country they believe will only deteriorate further. Consequently, despite the government's concerted efforts to encourage childbirth, the birth rate remains stagnant. Consequently, generational conflicts are becoming more prominent in Korea.

The previous list may give the impression that Korea is a really bad country. However, it's actually not that bad. It's difficult to quantify, but there are many positive aspects to Korea. (They are abundantly covered in the rest of this book, right?) Many societal systems are highly efficient, safety and security are top-notch, and the people are generally welcoming and amiable. Although living in a small country with few resources can be exhausting, Koreans possess a vibrant energy and know how to enjoy life. In ancient history books, Koreans are described as a people skilled at drinking, singing, and dancing. Furthermore, they are known for their friendliness towards foreigners. If you visit Korea, you'll experience many good things, and the people here will take care of any potential problems.

Lastly, I'd like to share two more interesting facts. The first one is about coins (real coins, not bitcoin). Korea is the world's leading producer of coin blanks, which are coins without any design or denomination. These coin blanks are exported to over 40 countries, making up approximately 50% of the global market share. It's fascinating to know that many countries, such as the United States, Europe, and Australia, use coins that originate from Korea.

Another fascinating fact is related to passport power. As of 2022, the South Korean passport holds an impressive position among the most powerful passports in the world. It grants visa-free access to an astounding 192 countries. This places Korea in second place, just behind Japan, which enjoys visa-free access to 193 countries. It's worth mentioning a noteworthy difference between the Korean and Japanese passports: Korean citizens require a visa to enter China, whereas Japanese citizens do not. (This may have a slight influence on the negative perception of China among Koreans. It's important to note that Chinese citizens also require a visa to enter Korea.) Furthermore, South Korea is a welcoming destination for citizens of 104 countries, as they can enter without a visa, ranking the country as the 37th most welcoming in the world.

# 10.
# Only Korea,
# Only Korean

_____

What's the deal with the grub they serve up to new moms in your countries? A refreshing beer to celebrate their well-deserved break? A comforting steak to lift their spirits? Like, if you're in the Netherlands, you'll be enjoying beschuit met muisjes(rust with mice), and in Turkiye, it's all about that lohusa serbeti(postpartum sherbet). Other nations got their own sparkling food for the occasion. But those foods are usually just one-time deals, serving as symbolic gestures with blessings or well-wishes. In Korea, they take things to the next level. New moms get to slurp down the same dish for every meal, day in and day out, for two to three weeks straight. And what's this magical dish that Korean moms can't get enough of, you ask? None other than "miyeok-guk", sea mustard soup.

Do people in your country have any particular foods they like to chow down on to celebrate birthdays? Now, if you're from the land down under or the Kiwi country, you probably think of fairy bread, and if you're Swedish, maybe you've got princess cake on your mind. And in China, there's a noodle called longevity noodle that's believed to bring good luck. For the most part, birthday specialties around the world tend to be desserts. However, Korea breaks the mold. On their birthdays, Koreans must slurp on some sea mustard soup. In Korea, the phrase "I didn't even get to eat sea mustard soup." is used as an idiom to describe a 'lonely birthday' or 'poorly celebrated birthday.'

Miyeok, also known as sea mustard, is a type of seaweed that holds sizable culinary importance in Korea. While many countries incorporate edible seaweed into their cuisine, none quite rival the consumption of seaweed in Korea. Koreans have a diverse range of seaweed dishes and consume it in substantial quantities. Miyeok is a prime example of the favored seaweed, but there are several others. One Korean seaweed variety that has garnered international recognition is "gim," also referred to as laver. (We will explore laver in more detail later on.)

Miyeok offers a variety of culinary possibilities beyond its usage in soup. In Korea, it can be enjoyed straight from the sea, often paired with a dipping sauce called "chogochujang." This spicy sauce is made with gochujang, sugar, and vinegar. This dipping sauce is also used as a condiment for Korean sashimi. Its appearance may resemble ketchup, but with a appealing spiciness. Another enticing way to savor miyeok is in the form of a salad when paired with the appropriate dressing. However, the traditional method of preparing miyeok in Korea is through making miyeokguk. This involves soaking and cooking dried miyeok instead of using fresh sea mustard. While beef is the most common ingredient used in miyeokguk, various types of seafood such as clams, abalone, oysters, and fish can also be used to create this flavorful soup.

While it may seem unusual to have sea mustard soup as a staple meal for several weeks after giving birth, what's even more unique is the location where it's consumed. In Korea, the majority of mothers give birth in hospitals and are then transferred to a "sanhujoriwon," or postpartum care center, instead of going home immediately. It is estimated that approximately 80% of

Korean mothers spend two to three weeks at these centers to receive specialized postpartum care before returning home with their newborns.

The practice of "sanhujori" is a deeply ingrained tradition in Korea and is taken very seriously as part of the postpartum care routine. During this time, it is believed that the mother needs to rest and recover for a few weeks after giving birth. In Korea, there is a strong belief that proper postpartum care is essential for a mother's well-being, and a lack of it may lead to potential health problems in the future. However, it is important to note that there is limited scientific evidence to support these widespread beliefs.

In the past, during the postpartum period, the mother was often relieved of domestic duties and was not solely responsible for taking care of the child. Instead, it became the responsibility of the entire family to support and care for both the mother and the newborn. This practice allowed the mother to focus on her recovery and bonding with the baby. Unfortunately, not all women had access to such support and some may have been subjected to inconsiderate treatment from their husbands or in-laws, compelling them to undertake strenuous tasks shortly after giving birth.

However, in the age of the nuclear family, finding someone to help with postpartum care has become increasingly challenging, leading to the rise of postpartum care centers as an alternative. These centers emerged in the mid-1990s and have since become widespread. Mothers choose to stay at these centers to rest, breastfeed their babies, engage in exercise programs, receive massages, and form friendships with other mothers who have recently given birth. These newfound friendships often extend beyond the center, resulting in postpartum reunions that can last for years. Husbands typically visit after work to spend time with their children and wives.

These postpartum care centers are not government-funded or covered by insurance. Instead, individuals are required to pay for the services in full. The cost of staying at these centers is higher than that of a standard hotel stay, as it includes accommodation, three meals a day, childcare service, and a range of additional amenities. The price for a two-week stay usually amounts to around $2,000, varying depending on the location and facilities of the center. Opting for a suite can increase the cost to well over $3,000, with the most luxurious options reaching upwards of

$10,000.

If you have a desire to taste sea mustard soup while in Korea, it can be a bit of a game of chance. While there are a few specific restaurants, primarily located in coastal cities, which specialize in different types of sea mustard soup, some restaurants in Seoul offer it as a side dish alongside many other options. In such cases, the portion size may not be substantial, and the flavor may not be particularly outstanding.

Anyway, despite its association with birthdays, sea mustard soup remains a beloved dish in Korea and is commonly enjoyed beyond special occasions. If you're eager to try it and don't have the opportunity to visit a restaurant that serves it, you can still experience the flavors by purchasing ready-made sea mustard soup from convenience stores. These pre-packaged options simply require you to add hot water or microwave them for a few minutes, providing a convenient way to enjoy this authentic Korean dish.

The love for sea mustard soup among Korean mothers is indeed special. It is said that even those who don't typically enjoy it find themselves consuming it, in spite of being boring. Sea mustard soup may hold a symbolic significance as a ritual, a way of praying for the health and happiness of a newborn baby. According to legend, the success of the Cha Hospital Group, which started as a single maternity clinic and has now expanded to include multiple large hospitals, medical schools, and related businesses, can be attributed to the "delicious sea mustard soup" served to new mothers. (Even the Los Angeles branch of Cha Hospital serves it to new mothers.)

The reason behind insisting on mothers to eat sea mustard soup is still not entirely clear, but there are some theories. One of them is that the soup's high iodine content is beneficial for the mother and the child's health. However, it's worth noting that excessive iodine intake can cause or exacerbate thyroid problems and other issues, as cautioned by doctors. Another likely but unfounded explanation is that it is a matter of convenience for the person responsible for cooking during the postpartum period, such as the mother or mother-in-law, who may find it laborious to prepare a new side dish for each meal.

It is indeed amusing to note that in Korea, there is a custom of avoiding sea mustard soup during exams. This is due to the slimy texture of sea mustard, as the Korean word for "slip" is associated with negative connotations related to exam failure.

Instead, people often choose foods such as "chabssaltteog," a glutinous rice cake, or "yeot," a rice taffy, which have a sticky texture. This preference is influenced by the positive associations of the Korean word for "stick" with passing an exam.

Korean wedding and funeral customs differ from those of other cultures. In Korea, guests are expected to give money as a gift for both ceremonies and the amount varies depending on the relationship and financial means of the guest. Typically, it's common to give $50 or $100 in an envelope. (If someone is unable to attend the wedding or funeral in person, it's common for them to pass on their monetary gift to another attendee or to pay online.) Attendance is also much higher than in other countries, with hundreds of people often attending, and over a thousand people may attend if the individuals involved have high social status. (Weddings are generally an hour-long ceremony and require a large space, while funerals last for two nights and three days and require less space.) The scale of these events can make them quite costly, which can be a burden for most people. To alleviate the burden, there is a culture of acquaintances contributing little by little to the cost. Although there are ways to have a smaller ceremony and not exchange moneys, it's difficult to change the culture once it's formed.

Another intriguing aspect of Korean weddings is the concept of "guest jobs." In Korean culture, it is considered embarrassing to have a wedding with too few guests. Therefore, if the number of invitees falls short for any reason, people may opt to pay a small fee to bring in fake guests. While this practice is not very common, it is not unheard of either. In the movie "Parasite," actress Park So-dam's character mentioned her past experience with "hired wedding guest."

It is noteworthy to highlight another exceptional aspect of funerals in Korea: the common practice of locating funeral homes within hospitals. In Korea, funeral services typically span a period of three days, attracting a considerable number of guests who come to offer their condolences. In the past, funerals were often conducted in private homes. However, as societal dynamics have evolved, it has become increasingly challenging to host funerals at home, leading to the establishment of dedicated funeral facilities. Given that many individuals pass away in hospitals, having funeral homes in close proximity has become convenient. While the idea of having a funeral home within a hospital may seem unusual to some foreigners, Koreans view it as a natural arrangement. It is worth mentioning that these funeral facilities are usually situated in discrete areas of the hospital.

One of the distinguishing characteristics of the Korean real estate rental culture is the practice of "jeonse." In Korea, there are two primary types of housing rentals: monthly rentals, which are common in other countries, and jeonse, which involves paying a considerable deposit to the landlord and not paying any monthly rent for the duration of the contract, commonly two years. At the end of the contract, the tenant receives their deposit back in full. In the case of jeonse, the deposit amount is substantial, often exceeding half the price of the house. For example, for a $1 million house, the deposit would range between $500,000 and $700,000. (Is the price of $1 million for the house described in the example considered too high? Due to Korea's limited land area and dense population, real estate prices, particularly in Seoul, are generally high. It is not uncommon for a small 100-square-meter apartment to cost over $1 million, and homes in certain neighborhoods may range from $3 million to $4 million or even higher.) While the jeonse system may appear straightforward, it can be complex, especially in Seoul where the demand for housing is intense, and real estate prices are continuously rising. The Korean government has made efforts to address the issues associated with the jeonse system in recent decades, but the controversy surrounding it remains unresolved.

The "banjiha" or semi-basement housing is indeed a notable aspect of real estate in Korea. These homes are situated with their floors more than a meter below ground level, while the windows are positioned above ground, allowing occupants to have a view of the outside. Usually, these houses are occupied by low-income families. However, banjiha housing often faces issues such as dampness and mold, leading to a characteristic odor that can cling to clothes and skin. The portrayal of this type of housing in the movie Parasite brought attention to its unique characteristics and living conditions.

Semi-basement housing has a historical and cultural context that dates back to the late 1960s. In 1968, a group of North Korean special force operatives infiltrated Seoul with the aim of assassinating the president. Out of the 31 operatives, 28 were killed, two managed to escape to the North, and one was captured alive. The captured operative eventually returned to South Korea, became a pastor, and now lives in the country at the age of 80s. While the operation ultimately failed, the event left a deep impact on South Korean society. Later, in the 1970s, during a time when tensions between North and South Korea were high(much higher than they are now), the South Korean government made it mandatory for every home to have a basement as a precautionary measure in case of war. Originally, it was illegal to rent out these underground spaces, but in the 1980s, as the housing shortage became more severe, regulations were relaxed and semi-basement housing became home to many low-income families.

Although the number of semi-basement houses in Korea is decreasing, there are still around 320,000 of them, with over 60% of them located in Seoul. The severe flooding caused by the heaviest rainfall in over a century in the summer of 2022 resulted in significant damage, with a particularly devastating impact on these homes, causing deaths. The water flooding scene in Parasite, which served as an excellent metaphor for the wealth inequality in Korean society, tragically became a reality in 2022.

Surrogate driving is a unique practice in Korean culture where a person can hire a driver to operate their car after they have been drinking. The service is very popular in Korea, where drinking is relatively tolerated. The price is usually higher than a one-way taxi fare and lower than a round-trip taxi fare. If you've been drinking in front of work, it's more economical to use a surrogate driving service than to park your car, take a taxi home, and then take a taxi to work the next morning. However, it can be challenging to find drivers between 10 p.m. and midnight due to the high demand. In the pre-smartphone era, drivers were called by phone, and now most people use apps. Such services exist in some foreign countries, including Okinawa in Japan, but they are not as common as they are in Korea.

Koreans have characteristic customs surrounding alcohol. One such custom is the belief that alcohol should be served to each other. So, it is occasionally considered somewhat impolite or improper not to refill someone's glass after they have emptied it, or to pour a drink for oneself. In bars, it is common for some-one to ask, "Are you busy?" out of the blue, which is a playful way of saying, "Are you so busy you don't have time to pour me a drink?" When someone pours a drink, it is important to accept it with a glass in hand. Between friends, one hand is acceptable for pouring or receiving drinks, but if pouring for someone in authority or receiving drinks from someone in authority, two hands should be used. There was also a custom of "sharing the glass", although this is gradually disappearing due to hygiene concerns. This is the act of emptying one's own glass (after pretending to wipe it formally with a tissue) and then holding it out to the other person to pour them a drink. It's interpreted as a sign of intimacy, but many people don't like this custom.

It's quite surprising that there are a number of unique Korean foods you won't find anywhere else in the world. (Think about it - can you name a food that's exclusive to your country and not enjoyed anywhere else on the planet? It's a rare find, but Korea has several such dishes. What a diversity of Korean food culture!) While a few of these might seem unconventional in looks or taste, making them somewhat challenging for foreign palates, most can be sampled by newcomers without much fuss.

One fruit that's worth trying in Korea is "chamoe", a type of Korean melon. This exotic fruit features a vibrant yellow skin and white flesh, falling between the size of a cantaloupe and an apple. While its flavor resembles that of a melon, chamoe possesses its own distinctive taste that sets it apart. It's not easy to find outside of Korea, and if you do spot it in some countries, chances are it was imported from Korea. If you visit Korea during the summer, be sure to give chamoe a try.

Next, we have "kkaennip," also known as perilla leaf. While sesame is a well-known ingredient, kkaennip must be less familiar. You probably don't know anyone who hasn't shouted "Open sesame" at least once as a child, inspired by the story of "Ali Baba and the Forty Thieves" from One Thousand and One Nights. (There's also the globally successful children's program Sesame Street.) Also, sesame has been around long enough to be one of the first crops humans cultivated for oil. Although it may not be as commonly used in the West, sesame oil is a crucial ingredient in East Asian cuisine, including Korean dishes like bibimbap, which you've most likely tried.

Perilla seeds, similar in appearance to sesame seeds but particularly distinct, have an exclusive place in South Korean cuisine. Despite their visual resemblance to sesame, these seeds belong to a different botanical category. While shiso is appreciated in Japan, and coriander or cilantro is commonly used in Southeast Asian dishes, perilla stands apart. This exceptional plant is versatile in its usage, setting it apart from its culinary counterparts. Sesame seeds can be enjoyed whole or pressed into oil. Shiso and cilantro are primarily cherished for their leaves. On the other hand, perilla offers a range of culinary possibilities. Its seeds can be consumed directly or pressed for oil, while its leaves are equally delectable. Roasted perilla seeds, when ground into a powder, serve as a characteristic spice in many Korean dishes. However, the crowning glory of perilla lies in its leaves, a culinary treasure unique to Korean traditions. Interestingly, many Koreans may not even be aware that these leaves are exclusive to Korean cuisine. In fact, some mistakenly believe they are eating sesame leaves. This confusion might arise because sesame oil is much more prevalent than perilla oil, but it's important to note that sesame leaves aren't a part of the Korean culinary repertoire either.

If the term "kkaennip" sounds familiar, you're certainly diving deep into this book. If you can even pinpoint where you encountered it, your memory is quite outstanding. It was introduced earlier as one of the vegetables commonly paired with pork belly. While it might not boast the same level of fragrance as shiso or cilantro (a point Japanese and Vietnamese individuals might contest), or the robust aroma of Western herbs like thyme, rosemary, parsley, and basil (though Westerners may have a different perspective), perilla leaves are certainly worth a try. At first bite, you might think you're just chewing on a leaf and wonder why you're eating it. But, as you savor the experience and take your time, you will discover a subtle flavor with a hint of mint and a gentle bitterness. Rest assured, perilla leaves are perfectly safe to consume. So go ahead and give them a try!

Koreans have a wide range of culinary applications for perilla leaves. They are commonly paired with grilled meats and sashimi, adding a fresh and aromatic element to the dishes. Perilla leaves are also used in salads, stews, and soups, enhancing the overall flavor profile. Additionally, perilla leaves are utilized in the preparation of kimchi or pickles, serving as a flavorful and aromatic side dish. When dining at a Korean restaurant, you'll frequently find perilla leaves used in a variety of dishes.

Besides, Koreans enjoy a variety of exclusive dishes not found elsewhere. One such delicacy is "golbaengi," also known as moon snail. Golbaengi is a well-liked drinking snack and can be compared to the Korean version of escargot. Another unusual ingredient is "dotori," which translates to acorn. In Korea, acorns are transformed into "muk," a type of jelly that serves as a side dish or snack, often enjoyed with alcohol. Dotori-muk resembles brown pudding and is commonly eaten using chopsticks, showcasing the dexterity of Koreans who are known for their excellent chopstick skills. "Kongnamul," or soybean sprouts, is another unique food in Korean cuisine. While similar to the mung bean sprouts consumed in many other countries (of course including Korea), kongnamul has a slightly firmer texture. Koreans also have a tradition of incorporating various grasses and leaves into their meals.

Koreans have a remarkably diverse palate when it comes to vegetables, with more than 300 types being consumed at least occasionally. There's a lighthearted joke that goes: 'If Koreans don't eat a type of grass, it must be poisonous.' Not only do Koreans eat a wide variety of vegetables, but they also consume them in substantial quantities. Despite a considerable meat consumption, the obesity rate in Korea is lower compared to other countries. This could be attributed to the abundance and variety of vegetables in their diet.

Maybe, it can be hard for foreigners to understand how humans can eat so many different plants. The key to understanding the consumption of such a diverse array of vegetables lies in the variety of condiments used to enhance their flavors. Even plain, unremarkable vegetables can be transformed by dipping them in the aforementioned ssamjang or gochujang. Koreans will even enjoy boiled cabbage (as long as they have a ssamjang) or broccoli (as long as they have a gochujang). The addition of sesame oil further enhances the taste.

At this point, it's important to clarify the meaning of the word 'namul'. Namul refers to a wide range of human-edible grasses and leaves, as well as foods that are boiled, stir-fried, or served raw and seasoned. Most vegetables can be quickly blanched and dressed with doenjang or soy sauce and sesame oil to create a delicious side dish. Bibimbap, which we'll discuss later, consists of rice mixed with a variety of vegetables and seasoned with gochujang and sesame oil.

Lastly, here are a few "only Koreans eat" foods that you probably don't come across very often, or if you do, they're not easy to eat. Among these foods is "mideodeok," which is a stalked sea squirt found in coastal areas. It's a coastal invertebrate that doesn't look or taste great, but some people love it for its distinctive sea smell. Mideodeok is commonly used in steamed seafood dishes and doenjang jjigae, a traditional fermented soybean paste stew. Then there's "beondegi" which often puts off foreigners but enjoyed by Koreans as street food or as a snack with alcohol. Beondegi refers to silkworm pupae. It's worth noting that Koreans consume the pupae of a specific species, the silkworm, and not any other insects. Although they may resemble worms (it's natural because they are indeed worms), they have a pleasant taste if one can ignore what it is. However, not all Koreans enjoy this particular food.

There is a Korean dish called "san-nakji," which refers to live small octopus, that gained global awareness through the movie "Oldboy." However, it's important to note that Koreans do not consume it in the manner depicted in the movie. Instead, the small octopus is typically chopped up, seasoned with sesame oil and salt, and eaten. Although it may seem alive due to its movement, it is not. If you're hesitant to try it because of its appearance, you can wait until it stops moving, which usually happens quickly. Octopus, which is referred to as "mooneo" in Korean, is highly regarded in Korean cuisine, despite being referred to as a "devil fish" in some countries. In fact, its Korean name translates to "literature fish." Squid is of course a popular seafood in Korea, and there's also a very small version called "jukkumi" (webfoot octopus). Koreans enjoy all of these seafood delicacies, but octopus and small octopus tend to be more expensive, while squid and jukkumi are relatively affordable. If you're not inclined to try live small octopus, I recommend sampling the spicy stir-fried small octopus dish called "nakjibokkeum." It is known for its fiery spiciness and is sure to leave an impressive memory to you.

Lastly again, there is a Korean delicacy called "hongeo," which refers to skate, featured in the Netflix series "Narco-Saints"(although it is actually imported from Chile and Argentina, not Suriname). Skate caught off the coast of Korea is particularly expensive, with an 8-kilogram fish costing hundreds of dollars. Hongeo has one of the most distinguishable and powerful flavors among all Korean foods. When consumed raw, it possesses a strongly pronounced taste, but it is also fermented to intensify its flavor. If you can handle stinky tofu in China, durian in Southeast Asia, lutefisk in Northern Europe, and surströmming in Sweden, then you can certainly give Korean skate a try. Koreans often enjoy it with boiled pork and aged kimchi, which they refer to as "samhap," meaning three things together. It is estimated that approximately 40% of Koreans enjoy hongeo, 30% consume it occasionally but do not necessarily enjoy it, and 30% have never tasted it (this is just my estimation). Are you willing to go the extra mile and give it a try?

# 11.

# Hangeul: The Only Alphabet with a Known Inventor

Who on Earth invented the alphabet? Did Sergey Brin and Larry Page team up in some secret warehouse to create it? And if that wasn't the alphabet we're referring to, who was the genius that came up with the first (English) alphabet? Well, that remains a mystery for the ages! What we do know is that in ancient times, the Greeks drew great inspiration from the Phoenicians, which eventually led to the development of the alphabets we utilize today in some languages such as English.

Then, who invented Chinese characters? It's a question as intricate as the characters themselves. What we can gather is that rudimentary hieroglyphics existed in ancient times and gradually evolved into the complex writing system we know today. While it's clear that the Japanese kana script drew inspiration from Chinese characters, the exact origin story and timeline remain elusive. A similar enigma surrounds the scripts of many other languages and even the fascinating history of Arabic numerals.

The Korean alphabet, Hangeul, stands out as an amazing exception. It was created during the reign of King Sejong the Great in 1443, within the Joseon Dynasty. King Sejong didn't accomplish this monumental task single-handedly; it required years of dedicated effort from a group of talented scholars under his guidance. When we say 'King Sejong invented Hangeul,' we're not just paying him lip service, as his unwavering determination and support were instrumental in bringing this revolutionary and phonetic writing system to life. In fact, it is widely believed that King Sejong himself actively participated in its development.

Since ancient times, Koreans had their own language, but they encountered a major obstacle—they lacked a writing system of their own. Before the 15th century, only a small group of intellectuals relied on Chinese characters, while the majority of the population grappled with their ineffective use. Even those who devoted themselves to studying Chinese characters found it challenging to apply them to the Korean language. The fundamental differences between Chinese and Korean were apparent. As a result, the language experience for all Koreans was marked by discomfort and inconvenience.

Before the invention of Hangeul, intellectuals in Korea dedicated themselves to the study of Chinese characters from a young age, much like how individuals today engage in learning foreign languages. They possessed the ability to decipher sentences written in Chinese characters and express their thoughts through writing using the same script. While their spoken language was Korean, their reading and writing skills revolved around Chinese characters.

However, only a select few were proficient in conversing in Chinese. When reading texts written in Chinese characters, they would pronounce the characters using Korean readings. Each Chinese character had its own Korean pronunciation, separate from its Chinese counterpart. Official examinations for government officials were conducted in Chinese characters, and all official documents were written using the same script. Poetry and novels were also composed in Chinese characters. Unfortunately, the majority of Koreans who were unable to learn Chinese characters faced significant challenges in acquiring new skills and effectively expressing their thoughts.

King Sejong the Great, the visionary fourth king of the Joseon Dynasty, had a profound desire to transform the linguistic landscape of Korea. His ambitious goal was to create a new writing system that would provide all citizens with easy access to literacy. However, this audacious undertaking encountered strong opposition from the intellectual circles of the time. There may have been diplomatic considerations, as it could potentially offend China, a nation that had exerted considerable influence over Korea for centuries, and there were also other reasons as below.

While the plight of the illiterate majority posed burdensome challenges, it should be noted that intellectuals well-versed in Chinese characters faced relatively fewer inconveniences. In fact, their command of Chinese characters conferred a sense of privilege to the intellectuals themselves, symbolizing their belonging to the ruling class and serving as a mechanism for upholding the existing social hierarchy. Their vehement resistance to the creation of a new writing system was precisely due to these vested advantages. The fear was prominent among the intellectual elite: a more educated populace, empowered by the acquisition of this new script, might lead to the erosion of their privileged positions, necessitating the relinquishment of some of their vested rights.

Undeterred by the resistance, King Sejong persevered and ultimately devised a new script that harmoniously complemented the Korean language. This revolutionary writing system was aptly named "Hun-min-jeong-eum," meaning "the correct sounds for the instruction of the people." The purpose behind its creation, proclaimed in the name of the king himself, encapsulated the very essence of King Sejong's spirit. "The language of Korea differs from that of China, rendering the written language incompatible and limiting the people's ability to effectively convey their thoughts and desires. This lamentable situation has moved me to create a fresh set of twenty-eight characters, designed to be easily learned and comfortably utilized by all individuals in their daily lives."

Indeed, when Hangeul was initially devised, it consisted of 28 letters—17 consonants and 11 vowels. Over time, four of these letters fell out of use, resulting in the current composition of 14 consonants and 10 vowels, totaling 24 letters. Although this may seem slightly fewer than the English alphabet, Hangeul's letters can be ingeniously combined to represent an extensive range of sounds, with specific methods for combining two consonants or including more than two vowels to represent certain sounds, resulting in a more extensive set of characters.

Korean is undeniably a challenging language for foreigners to learn, particularly for English speakers. However, amidst its complexity, Hangeul surprisingly emerges as a beacon of simplicity. Believe it or not, after just a week of dedicated study, one can grasp the ability to read Hangeul. Yes, you read that correctly! (However, this proficiency is limited to pronunciation itself and doesn't guarantee comprehension of meaning.)

The amazing simplicity of Hangeul arises from its consistent structure. Each letter in Hangeul is formed by combining a consonant and a vowel in one of two ways: either a consonant followed by a vowel or a consonant followed by a vowel and another consonant. This consistent combination method results in all Hangeul letters having a square shape. While these squares may bear some resemblance to Chinese characters, they are much simpler in nature. For foreigners, Chinese characters can often appear as intricate drawings or cryptic codes, whereas Hangeul takes the form of recognizable symbols or even logos.

A decade ago, Britney Spears made waves among Koreans when she donned a dress adorned with Hangeul, causing quite a stir. Perhaps, it's because in her eyes, Hangeul held a unique and distinct appeal as a design element. The fact that the seven characters on the dress were so unusual made it even more amusing. To draw an analogy, it could be likened to conveying 'a social group of Florida-born people living in Hollywood.' It wasn't actually referring to Hollywood or Florida, but rather a specific place name in South Korea. While I'm uncertain if such groups exist in abundance in other countries, Koreans have a propensity for forming such associations, as they often find a strong sense of connection in shared origins. Recently, there has been an increasing trend among foreigners to seek out fashion items incorporating Hangeul as a captivating design element.

Hangeul also offers great convenience when it comes to typing on computers or smartphones. With just 24 letters in the alphabet, which are repeated in assorted combinations of consonants and vowels, the typing process becomes straightforward. After placing one consonant and one vowel in each of the 26 spots in the English alphabet, you have two spots left. These two spaces are dedicated to the two most common complex vowels, which are written using two vowels. To type, you simply select the appropriate letters you need.

Hangeul's user-friendliness stems from its lack of case sensitivity and the absence of complex add-on symbols commonly found in European scripts. In comparison to many other languages that struggle to accommodate all their essential characters within the limited keyboard space and require multiple keystrokes or conversion keys for proper input, Hangeul emerges as one of the most efficient languages for keyboard input.

The repetition of consonants and vowels in Hangeul not only contributes to the ease of typing but also enhances typing speed. On the Hangeul keyboard layout, the majority of consonants are conveniently typed with the left hand, while most vowels are efficiently typed with the right hand. As a result, it is uncommon for a Hangeul typist to use either hand more than three times consecutively. In contrast, when typing in other languages, the use of the left and right hands can be irregular, and there are countless words that can be typed with only one hand, such as "water" and "million." Interestingly, there is one English word, "stewardesses," that requires using one hand a staggering twelve times in a row!

The advantage of Hangeul becomes even more pronounced when using a smartphone. While it is possible to type on a smartphone keyboard in a similar way to a regular keyboard, there are additional options available. This is because, while you still need 14 keys for 14 consonants, all of the vowels can be typed using just three keys!

King Sejong the Great, when creating Hangeul, designed the vowels using a combination of three elements: a dot, a horizontal line, and a vertical line. The dot represents the sky, the horizontal line represents the earth, and the vertical line represents the human. Although Hangeul's vowels may appear complex with their combination of horizontal and vertical lines, they can actually be simplified into short and long lines. Apart from one long line, which can be either horizontal or vertical, the other short lines can be considered as dots. (Although I'm trying to make it easy to explain, this may seem a bit perplexing for foreigners. For more information, you can search "Korean alphabet" on Alphabet's subsidiary, Google.) In practice, many Koreans can effectively type all of the vowels using just three letters, enabling them to text at an astonishingly high speed.

Hangeul is a source of immense pride for Koreans. If King Sejong the Great hadn't created Hangeul, Koreans would indeed still have to contend with the challenges of using a writing system that didn't align well with their spoken language. This would have made their linguistic situation even more complicated, especially considering the additional burden of learning English. That is why King Sejong the Great holds a revered place in Korean history, alongside General Yi Sun-sin. General Yi Sun-sin's remarkable achievements in defending against a Japanese invasion in the 16th century have made him another highly respected figure in Korean culture. The statues of both King Sejong and General Yi Sun-sin in Gwanghwamun Square, one of Korea's most significant locations, serve as powerful symbols of their importance. (The general stands, and the king sits behind.)

Additionally, King Sejong's contribution is commemorated by featuring him on the 10,000-won bill, which remained the highest denomination for an extended period until the introduction of the 50,000-won bill in 2009. Similarly, General Yi Sun-sin was honored on the now-discontinued five-hundred-won bill.

Speaking of which, let's explore some other Korean banknotes. The 1,000-won bill features the face of Joseon Dynasty scholar Lee Hwang (pen name Toegye), while the 5,000-won bill showcases Yi I (pen name Yulgok), another esteemed Joseon Dynasty scholar. On the 50,000-won bill, you'll find the face of Shin Saimdang, an influential figure in Korean history and celebrated poet, painter, and calligrapher. What's special about Shin Saimdang is that she is also celebrated for being the mother of Yulgok. This makes it the only banknote in the world to feature both a mother and son. (Interestingly, no mother and son have ever won a Nobel Prize, although Marie Curie and her daughter, Irène Joliot-Curie, were the first mother and daughter to receive a Nobel Prize.) If you're a fan of Korean actor So Ji-sub, you might find it intriguing to collect a 1,000-won bill as a souvenir, as there has been buzz about the striking resemblance between Toegye's portrait and So Ji-sub, particularly in the eyes.

Indeed, the creation of Hangeul was not the only remarkable achievement of King Sejong. Throughout his 32-year reign (1418-1450), he accomplished much more. He expanded the territory slightly to the north, establishing the borders of what is now the entire Korean Peninsula. King Sejong implemented various legal reforms and made significant contributions to agriculture and science. Notably, his reign witnessed the creation of the world's first rain gauge and the establishment of Korea's unique real estate leasing system, the Joense. King Sejong's dedication to improving the human rights of the people is exemplified by his comprehensive survey of the entire nation. In short, King Sejong is highly regarded as a transformative king who propelled Joseon, a budding nation, to multiple levels of progress simultaneously. Many Koreans believe that if there had been one or two more kings like King Sejong, the history of Joseon would have taken a drastically different path.

The name "Sejong" holds great prominence across the nation, being widely used in various contexts. Sejongno (Sejong Street), the expansive road in front of Gwanghwamun Gate, stands as a notable landmark bearing the name. Adjacent to it is Sejong Center, a large theater that showcases a wide array of cultural performances. Additionally, Sejong's legacy extends to the establishment of Sejong Special Self-Governing City, a new city that accommodates many of Korea's major government agencies. Moreover, the name "Sejong" finds its place in an array of institutions, including universities, hotels, and more.

However, one aspect that King Sejong the Great did not incorporate into Hangeul was the use of spacing between words. This omission could be attributed to the influence of the Chinese language, which customarily lacks clear spacing between characters. The absence of word spacing in Hangeul may have hindered its adoption in the centuries following its creation, beside the deliberate disregard for Hangeul by the ruling class of that time. It wasn't until the late 19th century, more than 400 years after the creation of Hangeul, that the practice of using spacing between words became widely embraced by Koreans. The introduction of word spacing greatly enhanced readability and played a pivotal role in facilitating Hangeul as a writing system.

Now, let's delve into another fascinating aspect of the Korean language – their intricate system of honorifics. While other languages incorporate honorifics, the Korean system is incredibly comprehensive. Hold on as we explore it – not only do they employ additional words for age, names, birthdays, and meals when speaking formally, but even common verbs like eat, ask, sleep, give, die, and say have varying forms. And that's not all; adjectives like hungry, personal pronouns, and titles are also part of this system.

Here's the entertaining part – they don't just have one or two honorifics for a given word, but a range of them! In the Joseon Dynasty, they even had a specific honorific reserved exclusively for the king. And the complexities continue in contemporary Korean society, where appropriate honorifics vary across different levels of hierarchy, ranging from top positions like chairman to managerial roles, from wise elder figures to friendly uncles, and many more.

Even in situations where there isn't a dedicated term, the Korean language provides multiple methods to convey honorifics. Honorific expressions are frequently found in postpositions that follow nouns, and you can even adjust verb and adjective endings to create honorific forms. I must say, it can be quite a challenge. (Although for us Koreans, it's not so difficult.) That's why it always impresses Koreans when they hear a foreigner expertly using honorific language.

In Korean culture, casual speech is predominantly reserved for very close relationships, while honorifics are commonly used in most other interactions. It is considered impolite not to use honorifics when meeting someone for the first time, irrespective of the age or status difference. However, there are a few situations where one might choose to use more casual language or speak without honorifics. Picture this: a bully picking a fight, a rogue mugger ready to snatch your wallet, or the dramatic encounter with a lifelong enemy. That's why many of the basic Korean phrases found in travel guidebooks are presented in honorific form - greetings, expressions of gratitude, requests, and so on. (Nevertheless, when foreigners don't use honorifics, Koreans are often amused to hear them because they understand that it's not an indication of hostility, but rather a limitation in their Korean language proficiency.)

The development of honorifics in the Korean language can be attributed to the cultural emphasis on hierarchy, which has been prevalent throughout Korea's history. A caste system has played a significant role, placing great importance on age-based hierarchy, even within the same caste. To exaggerate slightly, when Koreans encounter a stranger, there is a tendency to establish a hierarchy by first determining their respective ages. This is because the older individual has the liberty to speak casually, while the younger person is obligated to show respect. In modern society, however, even with an age difference, it is generally expected for individuals to maintain a respectful demeanor unless they share a close relationship or the younger person explicitly grants permission to use informal language.

Lastly, besides basic greetings, let me share a few entertaining Korean expressions that I believe foreigners traveling to Korea might find enjoyable to use. We've already covered phrases like "tesla" and "amugona," so here are a few more to add to your linguistic repertoire.

First, let's delve into the word 'yeogiyo.' It's formed by combining two words: 'yeogi,' meaning "here," and 'yo,' which is often added to express respect. This phrase proves useful when you want to call out to a staff member in a restaurant (I'll explain the reason behind this in the next chapter) or when you seek the attention of a stranger, similar to saying 'Excuse me.' By using 'yeogiyo,' you are essentially conveying the message, "Please pay attention to me here."

Let's move on to the word 'matjip.' Translated literally as 'taste-house,' it refers to a restaurant that serves mouthwatering, delectable food. Imagine this: you're dining at a restaurant, and the flavors tantalize your taste buds, leaving you thoroughly impressed. In that moment, you can turn to the waiter and exclaim, 'Yeogi matjibine!' The Koreans around you will be amazed at your Korean language skills and break into smiles. For an extra touch of excitement, don't forget to accompany your words with a thumbs-up gesture. It's the perfect way to express your satisfaction and share in the joy of experiencing exceptional cuisine.

Here's another expression for you to try out: 'daebak.' This versatile word carries the meaning of 'awesome,' 'jackpot,' or 'amazing,' making it the perfect choice when you want to convey your excitement about an extraordinary experience during your travels in Korea. Picture this: you've just finished an incredible meal at a restaurant, and it has left you thoroughly impressed. Instead of bidding a regular goodbye in Korean (which can be a bit harder to remember), you can leave with a memorable parting phrase: 'Daebak naseyo!' This phrase conveys the well-wish of 'May your business be successful,' showing your appreciation and goodwill to the establishment.

May you have the opportunity to explore and indulge in the finest restaurants in Korea, uttering the word "daebak" with great frequency. May your life be brimming with extraordinary and awe-inspiring moments, much like the essence of "daebak."

And lastly, I hope you will extend your support and blessings to this book, allowing it to achieve its own "daebak."

# 12.

# Unveiling the Marvels of Korean Restaurant Culture

We've already revealed some of the intriguing aspects you'll encounter in Korean restaurants. From the sneaky spoons and chopsticks hidden in secret compartments beneath the table to the blazing charcoal grills or sizzling burners at the center of your table, ready for your food-grilling adventures. And of course, the astonishing array of never-ending "side dishes" that appear without you even ordering them. But buckle up, because Korean restaurant culture is about to take you on a culinary journey like no other. Get ready for a truly unique dining experience!

For centuries, Koreans have embraced the profound traditions of Confucianism, a comprehensive philosophy, discipline, and religion. Confucianism has had a huge impact on Eastern culture as a whole, but its impact on people's real lives has been exceptionally deep-rooted, even surpassing its birthplace, China. This enduring influence can be attributed to the Joseon Dynasty, which upheld Confucianism as the nation's governing ideology for over five centuries.

While Confucianism espoused humanistic values, it also embraced strong patriarchal characteristics and placed great emphasis on rituals. Ceremonies, such as weddings and funerals, followed strict protocols, and ancestral rites were performed multiple times a year to honor departed spirits. Countless other rules dictated when and how certain actions should be performed, often lacking clear explanations. Nevertheless, as time progressed, many of these rules came to be seen as unnecessary and impractical in the modern world. So, since the mid-20th century, the Korean government has recognized these superfluous practices as "empty formalities and vanity," taking steps to reduce their prevalence. While their influence has gradually waned, remnants of this tradition still linger in a multitude of aspects of Korean society.

However, it is important to note that the strict adherence to Confucian rituals was primarily limited to the ruling class known as the "yangban." The common people, who made up the majority of the population, were not as bound by these rigid rules. Due to economic constraints, they often couldn't afford the elaborate rituals and saw little incentive to conform to customs that lacked legal requirements. Unlike the privileged ruling class deeply entrenched in Confucian tradition, ordinary Koreans exhibited an eminently pragmatic mindset. With a "why not?" mentality, they forged their own path and devised practical solutions for their daily lives.

One remarkable example of their ingenuity is the creation of singular tools. For instance, the "homi" is a Korean hand plow that is widely recognized for its efficiency in gardening. Koreans have also developed and introduced other innovative tools, such as the nickel-silver pot, which heats up quickly and cools down rapidly, and the "dolsot," a stone pot that heats up slowly but retains heat for an extended period. Despite not gaining widespread fame, there are many individuals who craft their own specialized tools tailored to their specific needs. Koreans truly embody the spirit of "homo faber," the maker of things.

It is conceivable that Koreans have developed a penchant for consuming a diverse range of vegetables and seafood compared to their foreign counterparts, potentially as a response to historical food shortages. While this notion is speculative and lacks scholarly support, it suggests that pragmatism runs deep in their cultural DNA, enabling them to adapt and employ various tactics and strategies for survival, whether through resourceful measures or the occasional gimmick.

Korea's distinctive restaurant culture has evolved through the accumulation of a variety of tricks aimed at enhancing efficiency. As previously emphasized, Korea experienced significant economic challenges in the not-so-distant past. During this period, individuals were reluctant to spend exorbitant amounts on meals. The populace sought a balance between high-quality dining experiences and affordability, prompting restaurant proprietors to devise ways to offer their guests at competitive prices, thereby attracting a larger customer base.

Consider this: It is undeniably more cost-effective to pre-set a multitude of forks, knives, and spoons on the table, allowing customers to conveniently utilize the utensils they require, rather than meticulously arranging them before each patron's arrival.

In the past, Korean restaurants used to store their cutlery in plastic or wooden containers, sometimes vertically positioned in elongated cylinders without lids. While this approach proved efficient, it posed two predicaments. Firstly, it compromised hygiene, particularly when using uncovered containers. Secondly, it cluttered the table with a conspicuous bin of cutlery.

Then, an ingenious Korean innovator, whose identity remains unknown, devised a solution: hiding the cutlery bin beneath the table's surface. Initially, only spoons and chopsticks found their discreet abode there. However, it soon became evident that this innovative concept could accommodate additional items. Napkins, bottle openers, and more discovered their rightful place in the concealed compartment. Koreans have an admirable openness to embracing exceptional ideas, and it didn't take long for this trend to gain traction. Now, countless restaurants feature tables adorned with this clever setup.

Consider the aspect of efficiency once more, this time in relation to the utilization of scissors. Imagine a sizable slab of succulent pork belly sizzling on the grill, and ponder the available alternatives. Given that Koreans predominantly employ spoons and chopsticks during their meals, resorting to a separate fork and knife for cutting the meat proves less than ideal. Additionally, with an array of delectable side dishes adorning the table, there is scarce space to accommodate such additional utensils. One could propose the notion of having a diligent waiter transport the cooked meat from you, subsequently slicing it in the kitchen, and finally returning it to your table. However, this approach proves laborious and impractical. So, why not endeavor to pre-cut the meat into bite-sized portions from the outset? Indeed, certain pork belly establishments adopt this practice. Yet, one may find it tiresome to incessantly flip over the diminutive meat pieces for thorough cooking.

Scissors come to the rescue, solving all your dilemmas. It's a breeze to wield a pair of scissors, effortlessly snipping through a moderately cooked slab of meat, allowing it to continue cooking to perfection. In upscale establishments, where the sizzling meat commands a higher price tag, the skilled staff expertly handles the cutting duties. However, in more casual eateries, it's common for patrons to take matters into their own hands and wield the scissors themselves.

In the realm of meat-cutting, scissors alone do not reign supreme; tongs also play a vital role. It is crucial to dispel any misconceptions that scissors are solely reserved for fabric or paper, for in the culinary world, their purpose takes on a different dimension. Koreans understand the significance of specialized tools, as they do not employ the same pair of scissors to conquer leather, manipulate wire, and slice succulent pork belly. Scissors designed explicitly for culinary endeavors are solely dedicated to the art of food cutting. Moreover, a subtle variation in their shape enhances their efficacy in this domain. The tips, intentionally blunted rather than pointed, and the blades, often subtly curved, epitomize the utmost convenience when it comes to the precise act of food cutting. So, next time you find yourself at a Korean barbecue restaurant, don't hesitate to grab those scissors and embark on a culinary adventure of meat-cutting mastery.

A true testament to our culture of efficiency is the ingenious invention known as the call bell. Found in many, though not all, restaurants, this small button discreetly positioned on the table or wall holds the power to fulfill your every desire. Whether you yearn for an additional serving of tantalizing meat, crave another round of invigorating soju, or find your kimchi bowl lamentably empty, a simple press of the button beckons a diligent server to your aid. The call bell effortlessly bridges the gap between customer and staff, ensuring a seamless and convenient dining experience for all.

Diners often find themselves with a myriad of requests to make while indulging in their meal. This is precisely why, in esteemed establishments, diligent servers make periodic visits to each table. They graciously attend to your needs, be it replenishing your water or wine, promptly replacing a dropped fork, swiftly clearing away empty plates, or even tidying up bread crumbs that may have found their way onto the table. Their attentive presence is not limited to your beckoning; they actively ensure your satisfaction by regularly checking in, even when unbidden. With a warm smile adorning their faces, they inquire about the quality of your dishes, your comfort level, and whether your desire additional orders. This exceptional level of service is driven by a twofold motivation: the pursuit of excellence in customer experience and the desire to maximize potential gratuities. That is to say, such exceptional service is not bestowed without its associated costs. Whether through gratuities or slightly elevated prices, you are offered the opportunity to appreciate and reciprocate the efforts of these dedicated individuals.

Restaurants in Korea have adopted an additional measure to

enhance their workforce efficiency by implementing call bells. This ingenious system alleviates the need for staff members to constantly monitor customers and enables them to attend to other tasks. With call bells at their disposal, patrons no longer face the challenge of making eye contact with the staff. If assistance is required, a simple ring of the bell summons the attentive service of the staff. However, what if you find yourself in a dining establishment without a call bell? Fear not, for we have already addressed this in a previous chapter: a straightforward and widely used solution is to call out "yeogiyo" to get the attention of the staff.

It is true that South Korea does not have a widespread tipping culture. Perhaps that's the reason why the staff doesn't have their peepers glued to customers like a hawk. It's like pondering the age-old dilemma of which arrived on the scene first, the clucking chicken or the elusive egg. Unlike some other countries, tipping in restaurants or taxis is not customary in Korea. In the past, when cash transactions were more common, people occasionally said "keep the change," but the amounts were typically small, usually around 50 cents or less. With the shift towards cashless transactions, these small tips have become less common. In the realm of Korean customs, leaving a dollar for the hotel maid or tipping the luggage carrier is not the norm, though it remains an option. While cash exchanges are customary at weddings and funerals, the practice of tipping has not gained traction. This could be attributed to a preference for simplicity and a general aversion to needless complexities.

Tipping can indeed be a rather intricate affair. It requires careful consideration of the appropriate amount to give, rummaging through one's wallet for cash, and the constant worry of striking the right balance between being perceived as stingy or overly generous. The thought of calculating percentages like 15% or 18% can be quite bothersome, adding unnecessary complexity to the equation. How refreshing it is to simply pay the predetermined amount set by the business owner. As a recipient, there's no need to fret over receiving a smaller tip than expected or exhaust oneself in the pursuit of securing more.

In Korean restaurants, where the concept of tipping is not prevalent, the distribution of responsibilities among the staff is not rigidly defined. This flexibility allows anyone to attend to your needs based on the situation, leading to a more efficient system. Contrast this with the image of a restaurant in a country where a much larger portion of your tip goes directly to your designated server. In such cases, regardless of how many bustling staff members come and go around you (even when they are not so busy), if your server happens to be absent, it can cause inconvenience. In the absence of a designated server, you have the freedom to approach any staff member for assistance, knowing that your requests will be promptly attended to.

Indeed, when Koreans visit foreign countries with a tipping culture, they adhere to local customs and tip accordingly. "When in Rome, do as the Romans do" is a well-known maxim to all the Koreans. However, the process can feel unfamiliar and perplexing. It involves scrutinizing the menu prices, estimating the currency exchange rate, and factoring in the gratuity, making it challenging to determine the total cost of the food being ordered. The act of writing the tip amount on a credit card receipt can feel unsettling, too. Not only is the calculation process complex, but the notion of paying an additional 20% gratuity, which is non-existent in Korea, can leave one with a sense of being overcharged.

In most cases, tipping is not expected during your trip to Korea. However, it's worth noting that tipping is not entirely absent in the country. Some high-end restaurants, particularly those in upscale hotels, may include a 10% tip expectation on their menus. Moreover, in the following situations, tipping is sometimes expected (and recipients are usually very appreciative for the unexpected tips): when you receive exceptional service at a high-end beauty salon, when the staff at a premium beef restaurant skillfully prepares and grills your meat, when the owner-chef personally visits your table at a top-notch sushi restaurant and greets you with utmost politeness, when you're genuinely impressed with the food or service and wish to express your appreciation, or when you want to convey a generous and affluent image during a date or business meeting. It's important, however, not to be overly arrogant when tipping for any of these purposes, as it can have a negative impact.

In certain restaurants in Korea, it is not uncommon to find a roll of toilet paper placed on the table. While it may initially seem unusual to have restroom items alongside the food, it has a historical context rooted in economic hardships. Several decades ago, Koreans would use newspapers as makeshift toilet paper and keep the rolls of actual toilet paper in the living room or on the dining table for convenience. Although this practice is now rare in Korean households, some budget-friendly restaurants choose to provide rolled tissues instead of standard napkins as a cost-saving measure. So, if you happen to encounter this unique setup, there's no need to be surprised or concerned.

To keep costs down, many Korean restaurants adopt a "self-service" approach. It is not uncommon for these establishments to require customers to help themselves to water while serving the main dishes. Additionally, a notable feature is the availability of "side dishes," like kimchi, which are often offered as a self-serve buffet with unlimited refills. In certain cases, diners may be encouraged to enjoy self-served ice cream or coffee after the meal. By observing the behavior of others, you can easily navigate and adapt to these practices.

The most crucial step for diners in Korean restaurants is to set their own spoon and chopsticks. Unlike Western restaurants that commonly lay out utensils like forks and knives in a neat row, Korean restaurants (except high-class establishments) often hide spoons and chopsticks in a box beneath the table, leaving it to customers to retrieve and arrange them. However, simply leaving the utensils on the table is not the norm in Korean dining culture. It is ingrained in Korean etiquette that the majority of

Koreans will grab a napkin, place it on the table, and then position their cutlery on top of it. This practice serves a purpose, as tablecloths or mats are seldom changed between diners and are usually wiped down with a dishcloth, sometimes even sanitized with alcohol spray. Due to this, the tables may not always feel completely clean, so using napkins as makeshift disposable mats is a common practice. By following these practices, you can fully immerse yourself in the Korean dining culture.

Interestingly, it is quite common for the youngest person in a group to take on the responsibility of setting everyone's cutlery when dining at a restaurant in Korea. While it is not a strict requirement, many Koreans consider it a natural gesture rooted in the Confucian tradition of showing respect to elders. However, it is important for elders not to take this for granted. And then, they may be playfully referred to as "ggondae" or "boomer." It is advisable to either make an effort to set your own cutlery or express gratitude to the person who takes on the task. Similarly, when visiting samgyeopsal restaurant, it is often the duty of the youngest person to handle the grilling and cutting of the meat. (Of course, there may be exceptions, with some ggondae who particularly enjoys grilling taking charge. In such cases, it is appropriate to commend their grilling skills by saying something like, "Hey, manager, you're really good at grilling meat.")

Now that you're immersed in the Korean restaurant culture, you can fully embrace the experience. As soon as you take your seat at the table, even before placing your order, gracefully retrieve the napkins, spoons, and chopsticks from under the table and arrange them neatly. Don't forget to engage in the unique practice of cutting your food with scissors—it adds a touch of authenticity to your dining experience. And if you find yourself craving an extra bottle of soju, simply ring the bell, and a prompt and attentive staff member will swiftly come to your aid. Remember, tipping is not customary in Korean restaurants, but if you truly enjoyed your meal and wish to show appreciation, you can utilize the Korean phrases you've learned earlier. To express your satisfaction, shout out something like, "Daebak! Yeogi Matjibine!"

# 13.

# Noodlicious Obsession: Koreans' Passion for Noodles and Pot Liquor

In June 2022, South Korean newspapers highlighted a fascinating piece of information as follows. "South Koreans are the world's second-largest consumers of ramen noodles per capita. The World Instant Noodles Association (WINA) reported that in 2021, South Koreans consumed an average of 73 ramen noodle servings per person per year, placing them just behind Vietnam, which claimed the top spot with 87 servings. Nepal followed closely in third place with 55 servings. Remarkably, South Korea has been the number one position since 2013, when the statistics began, but it dropped to second place."

What caught the attention even more were the colorful comments from readers on the article. Expressions like "I'm weirdly pissed off," "I'm going to have one and a half servings from now on," "I'm furious," "I need to get my act together", and "I'm having ramen for lunch today" were just a few examples of the passionate responses. It's clear that ramen holds a special place in the hearts and stomachs of South Koreans, evoking a range of emotions and sparking enthusiastic discussions about personal ramen consumption habits. Without a doubt, Koreans take their ramen seriously.

Ramen, originally from China, found its true calling in Japan with a fascinating twist. While initially enjoyed in specialized restaurants, the advent of instant ramen in 1958 transformed it into a convenient meal that could be easily prepared at home. In the 1960s, the Korean peninsula caught wind of this culinary sensation when a South Korean company imported the Japanese technology, catapulting instant ramen to newfound popularity as an affordable and time-saving meal option. Since then, Korean ramen has undergone a flavor revolution, adapting to suit the discerning Korean palate. As a result, it has emerged as a bolder, spicier counterpart to its Japanese cousin, boasting a tantalizing array of flavors and varieties. So from now on, when we mention ramen, we're talking about the Japanese version, while "ramyun" takes center stage as the beloved Korean twist on this noodle sensation. (Actually, Koreans call the Japanese version "ramen" and the Korean version "ramyun".)

Korea is truly a paradise for instant ramyun enthusiasts. With a staggering selection of over 500 varieties available on the market today (and that's excluding discontinued ones), the options are virtually limitless. You'll find an array of noodle thicknesses, an assortment of soup base powders with different flavors, varying levels of pot liquor, and even influences from Chinese and Southeast Asian cuisines. While the standard cooking time is around four minutes of boiling, there's a whole range of ready-to-eat cup noodles that can be effortlessly prepared by adding hot water and waiting a mere three minutes. The spiciness spectrum of Korean ramyun knows no bounds, ranging from mild and non-spicy to tongue-scorchingly fiery.

The popularity of Korean ramyun extends far beyond the borders of Korea, with significant exports to international markets. In 2021 alone, the export value reached nearly $700 million, increasing to over $900 million in 2023. The allure of Korean ramyun can be attributed to its addictive nature, capturing the taste buds of people around the globe. Additionally, the rising global popularity of Korean content, including movies, music, and dramas, has also contributed to the increased demand for Korean ramyun overseas. In some instances, the creativity surrounding Korean ramyun knows no bounds. A prime example is the iconic dish Jjapaguri, featured in the critically acclaimed movie Parasite, where two different types of ramyun, Jjapaghetti and Neoguri, are ingeniously mixed together to create a peculiar and flavorful combination.

Koreans' deep affection for ramyun comes as no surprise, as it embodies several elements that resonate with their culinary preferences. Foremost, Koreans have an insatiable love for noodles, which is evident in the plethora of noodle dishes available, including the beloved cold noodles, "naengmyeon" that we'll delve into later. Additionally, Koreans have a special fondness for "gukmul," a term combining "guk" (soup) and "mul" (water). This refers to a watery part of stews of soup, besides the solid ingredients. It's worth noting that "gukmul" is also the name of BTS member Jin's pet sugar glider.

Koreans have a strong affinity for "gukmul" as an integral part of their meals. In contrast to Western dining practices, Koreans rarely consume water alongside their meals (although they do enjoy alcoholic beverages), choosing instead to incorporate varying amounts of soup. Notably, Korean soups tend to have a more subtle level of saltiness compared to their Western counterparts. In fact, when Koreans sample Western soups while traveling abroad, they often find them to be overly salty. However, despite the relatively lower salt content in Korean soups, the overall salt intake among Koreans remains high due to their much consumption of soup. In fact, Koreans have the highest salt intake globally, surpassing the recommended levels set by the World Health Organization by more than double.

Ramyun offers a multitude of advantages beyond its delectable taste. One of its greatest appeals is its affordability and swift cooking time, catering perfectly to the fast-paced lifestyle embraced by Koreans who live by the mantra "pali-pali" (quickly). Additionally, ramyun serves as a valuable resource for preventing hunger among those with limited means. While the noodles and soup alone provide a delightful culinary experience, you can further enhance your meal by incorporating additional ingredients such as eggs, green onions, ham, cheese, rice cakes, dumplings, and more, tailored to your personal preferences. It also pairs exceptionally well with the beloved Korean staple, kimchi. Moreover, it is not uncommon for many Koreans to add a small portion of rice to the soup after consuming all the noodles, elevating the dining experience to another level.

Occasionally, Koreans enjoy eating ramyun without boiling. That is, dry noodles are lightly seasoned with the soup powder and consumed as a snack or with alcoholic beverages. It's worth noting that the noodles are cooked once in the factory and then dried, allowing them to be eaten without additional cooking. This particular way of enjoying ramyun was depicted in the well-received drama "Squid Game," where actors Lee Jung-jae and Oh Young-soo were shown enjoying this style of ramyun while drinking soju in front of a convenience store.

The Korean expression for 'Do you want to Netflix and chill?' involves ramyun, which translates to 'Do you want to (come over my house and) eat ramyun?' This phrase gained popularity after actress Lee Young-ae, known for her roles in the drama 'Dae Jang Geum' (Jewel in the Palace) and the movie 'Sympathy for Lady Vengeance,' said it in the film 'One Fine Springday.' In the movie, the actor Yoo Ji-tae from 'Oldboy' was the recipient of the phrase. (Of course, their plans didn't end up being solely about eating ramyun.) While you may not have the opportunity to use this phrase in Korea, who knows what may happen in the world. Therefore, I wanted to share this magical expression with you in Korean. (How kind of me!) The pronunciation might not be perfect, but it can effectively convey your intention. Let's memorize it: "Ramyun meokko gallaeyo?"

With the abundance of delicious Korean food to try during your limited time in Korea, I wouldn't recommend relying solely on ramyun for your one meal. However, just like grabbing a late-night chicken snack, you might consider picking up some cup noodles from a convenience store on your way back to the hotel. If you find yourself overwhelmed by the extensive variety of ramyun options at the store, I suggest going for Shin Ramyun, which happens to be the top-selling Korean ramyun. Shin Ramyun is a bit on the spicy side, so if you're not a fan of spicy food, you can go with the second best-selling product, Jin Ramyun. (If you truly want to embrace the Korean experience, you can even grab the smallest size of kimchi.) If you enjoy it, be on the lookout for Korean Ramyun when you return to your home country; most large supermarkets and Asian food markets will have a selection of Korean ramyun available.

In addition to ramyun, there is a wide variety of noodle and broth dishes that Koreans hold dear. One of the most beloved among them is "naengmyeon", which translates to "cold noodles." Naengmyeon features a refreshing cold broth accompanied by noodles made from buckwheat. While there are various noodle dishes found worldwide, cold noodles are not common, and it's safe to say that none have achieved the same level of fame as naengmyeon. (Although it's worth mentioning that cold soba or udon noodles are consumed in Japan, they are typically enjoyed without a broth. The same goes for some noodle dishes that are widespread in Southeast Asia.)

Korea features a plethora of restaurants specializing in naengmyeon. While it can be challenging to determine an exact count due to many establishments serving a diverse range of dishes, including meat, that serve noodles too, it is estimated that there are over 20,000 restaurants nationwide that offer naengmyeon and other noodle delicacies. While some restaurants rely on factory-made broths, the most renowned and successful naengmyeon establishments prepare their own broth recipes and craft their noodles. Beef holds a pivotal role in naengmyeon broth, although some places incorporate chicken, chicken bones, pork, and other ingredients. Alongside meat, a variety of vegetables and fruits are commonly used as complementary components, and certain establishments even incorporate a broth made from water kimchi, a radish-based concoction without chili powder. The flavor profiles of naengmyeon can vary significantly from one restaurant to another, providing diners with a diverse and enticing culinary experience.

Indeed, there exist various types of naengmyeon, and the specific dish we have been discussing at length is called "pyeongyang naengmyeon." Its name is derived from Pyongyang, the capital city of North Korea, where it was originally created. The defining characteristic of pyeongyang naengmyeon is its "bland" broth. When Koreans try it for the first time, it is not uncommon for them to be taken aback by the apparent lack of flavor. Some even humorously describe it as if the chef decided to quit in the middle of cooking. The taste can vary from one restaurant to another, with some establishments emphasizing a particularly mild flavor profile. However, with repeated consumption, individuals often develop an appreciation for the subtle nuances of the light broth, eventually becoming avid fans of pyeongyang naengmyeon. Many people enjoy naengmyeon on a regular basis, with some even embarking on pilgrimages to celebrated naengmyeon restaurants throughout the country. In Korea, the question "Where is your favorite pyeongyang naengmyeon restaurant?" serves as a useful conversation starter and can lead to lively debates among individuals with differing taste preferences. It may be difficult to fully grasp the flavor after just one bite, but if you are a fan of the noodle dish, it is certainly worth a try. A list of particularly famous naengmyeon restaurants can be found at the end of this book.

There are other variations of naengmyeons worth mentioning. One notable type is "bibim naengmyeon", which consists of buckwheat noodles served without broth. Instead, they are topped with a spicy seasoning and enjoyed by mixing and rubbing the noodles with the seasoning, ensuring an even distribution of flavors. The term "bibim" is the same as the one used for "bibimbap," signifying the act of mixing and rubbing ingredients together. Another variation is "hoe naengmyeon", which incorporates slices of raw marinated fish tossed in spices alongside the noodles. These unique variations of naengmyeons are definitely worth trying during your second visit to Korea.

Another beloved Korean noodle dish is "kalguksu", which

derives its name from the combination of the words "kal" (knife) and "guksu" (noodle). This signifies that the noodles are originally handmade and cut with a knife, rather than being produced by a machine (although machine-made noodles have become more prevalent in recent times). The process of making kalguksu involves kneading flour, rolling it out, folding it with flour, and then cutting it with a knife, resulting in slightly coarse noodles. The soup for kalguksu commonly features ingredients such as beef, chicken, and shellfish, providing a flavorful and satisfying dining experience.

In addition to kalguksu, there is another Korean dish called "sujebi," which is similar in some ways but considered a seperate culinary creation. Sujebi is not technically a noodle dish. To make sujebi, you knead flour, let it rest for at least two hours, then roll it out by hand, cut it into small pieces, and drop it directly into boiling broth to cook. Think of it like making lasagna by hand, although sujebi does not contain eggs in the dough. The resulting texture of sujebi is smooth and charming. The broth for sujebi is prepared in a similar manner to kalguksu. However, kalguksu usually has a thicker broth due to the incorporation of flour from the noodles during the noodle-making process.

Kongguksu, or soy milk noodle soup, is another unique noodle dish that is exclusive to Korean cuisine. While the noodles themselves are plain, the soup is what sets it apart. To make the soup, soybeans are boiled and then ground in a blender (or traditionally using a millstone) with a small amount of water. The resulting mixture creates an exceptional and somewhat surprising taste. Despite its initial unfamiliar flavor (it's a little bit similar to but definitely different with soy milk), many Koreans consider kongguksu a delicacy with a long-standing tradition. The noodles are served cold, making it a particularly favored dish during the summer months.

There are several popular broth-based dishes in Korean cuisine. While kimchi-jjigae and doenjang-jjigae also have broth, the focus here is on dishes that have a significant amount of broth. Two well-known examples are "gomtang" and "seolleongtang". Both dishes are prepared by simmering beef for extended hours and served with rice, but they differ in their ingredients and resulting broth. Gomtang features a clear broth made solely from beef, while seolleongtang incorporates a combination of beef, beef organs, beef bones, and other elements, resulting in a cloudy broth. Additionally, some kind of gomtang can be prepared using specific parts of the cow, such as the tail or rumen.

"Haejangguk", also known as hangover soup, is a popular broth dish in Korean cuisine, specifically enjoyed as a remedy for hangovers. There are varying types of haejangguk, each with its own set of ingredients. Common components include bean sprouts, "ugeoji" (outer leaves of napa cabbage), and "seonji" (coagulated cow's blood). While the idea of consuming coagulated blood may sound unfamiliar to some, it is a flavorful element in the soup, and surprisingly, many foreigners also appreciate its taste.

There are several seafood broth dishes in Korean cuisine that are prepared by boiling and enjoyed for their flavors. When blue crab, known as "kkotge" in Korean, is added, it becomes "kkotgetang". Similarly, the addition of clams, known as "jogae", results in "jogaetang". And when various types of seafood are combined, it is called "haemultang", with "haemul" referring to seafood in general. Some other dishes commonly feature fish such as blowfish, cod, pollock, and others as the main ingredients. To enhance the flavors and reduce any fishy odors, a variety of vegetables are added, including "minari". Yes, that's the word in the movie title. In English, minari is translated as dropwort, water parsley, or water celery, but it is not widely appreciated outside of Korea.

There are a few more notable broth dishes in Korean cuisine. "Gamjatang" (pork back-bone stew) is prepared using pork vertebrae, potatoes, and veggies. On the other hand, "samgyetang" is a chicken soup infused with ginseng, where a whole small chicken is presented in a stone pot called "ttukbaegi". It may be surprising to see the chicken served whole, but you've known for a long time that chickens look like that. And rest assured, it does not include the head. The flavors of these dishes are truly marvelous. Gamjatang pairs exceptionally well with soju, making it a tempting combination worth trying if you have developed a fondness for the drink. Samgyetang is enjoyed throughout the year, but it holds particular popularity during the hot summer months when individuals seek a revitalizing boost for their bodies.

One more dish that should not be forgotten is "sundubu-jjigae", a spicy stew made with soft tofu. Sundubu-jjigae ranks third on the list of Koreans' favorite stews, just behind kimchi-jjigae and doenjang-jjigae. The key ingredient that sets it apart is the soft tofu (silken tofu), which has a wonderfully delicate texture. Sundubu-jjigae comes in diverse variations, with additional ingredients such as beef, pork, shrimp, oysters, clams, and octopus. What makes sundubu-jjigae truly absorbing is the way it is served. Typically, in Korean restaurants, you are served a variety of side dishes before the main course. However, in restaurants specializing in sundubu-jjigae, a raw egg is brought to the table. It's important to resist the temptation to crack the egg too soon or mistake it for a hard-boiled egg. When the piping hot stew arrives, still bubbling and simmering, you crack the raw egg into it and mix it in. The heat of the stew gently cooks the egg, creating a creamy and delicious addition to the already flavorful dish.

Yukgaejang, a spicy beef soup with vegetables, is another beloved Korean soup dish. This flavorful stew features tender beef and a medley of vegetables, including a staple ingredient called "gosari", which refers to fernbrake or bracken fiddleheads. Gosari is a unique vegetable primarily enjoyed by Koreans, and due to its poisonous nature, only the youngest stalks are harvested and cooked. In Korean cuisine, gosari is commonly consumed as "namul" and is also incorporated into dishes such as bibimbap and yukgaejang.

Introducing too many food options all at once may be overwhelming. Although I've tried to make it simple, it seems that I have confused you with too many food names. Given the limited time of your visit to Korea, it's impossible to try them all. Without further ado, here are some tips help your choice.

Of all the foods mentioned in this article, your first priority should be trying naengmyeon. If possible, visit an eminent restaurant to taste the authentic version. Wondering what to try next? If you enjoy beef consommé, venture into gomtang. For fans of pork stew, gamjatang is a must-try. If you're a noodle aficionado visiting Korea in the summer, kongguksu should be on your list. Had a bit too much soju yesterday? Haejangguk is your remedy. To experience exceptional ingredients you've never tried before, opt for haejangguk with seonji. Craving spice? Give yukgaejang or sundubu-jjigae a shot. If you're seeking an unconventional and Instagram-worthy food photo, samgyetang is a great choice. (Samgyetang is undoubtedly one of the top Korean dishes that Koreans enthusiastically recommend to foreigners.) Oh, the agony of a life devoid of precious ramyun time!

You might already be overwhelmed with the multitude of

food options you want to try, leaving you indecisive about what to choose. However, there are still numerous incredible Korean dishes that haven't been mentioned yet (some of which will be discussed later). Here's my advice for the hesitant ones: consider extending your stay in Korea by at least one more day, allowing yourself the opportunity to savor three additional culinary wonders.

# 14.

# Bibimbap and Street Food Extravaganza

You might think you already know a thing or two about Korean food, don't you? You might be scratching your head, wondering why I haven't talked about the big dogs yet: bulgogi, galbi, and bibimbap. Well, let me tell you, there's a method to our madness. These dishes are so well-known by foreigners and are available in Korean restaurants worldwide, so I figured, why bore you with something you already know? (Of course, indulging in Korean cuisine directly in Korea surpasses the experience of dining at a Korean restaurant abroad.) In this post, I'll dive into these classics and unravel the fascinating stories behind various Korean foods.

Let's kick things off with bulgogi, a dish whose name simply means grilled meat(gogi) over a fire(bul). While grilling meat is a universal practice, what sets Korean bulgogi apart is the magic that happens when thin slices of meat marinated in a savory soy sauce-based concoction. This perfect marriage of salty and sweet flavors has turned it into a darling among foreigners and one of the most sought-after Korean dishes.

Bulgogi is commonly crafted with beef, but it can also be prepared with pork, known as dwaeji-bulgogi, to avoid any confusion. In the case of pork bulgogi, the seasoning often incorporates gochujang, adding a spicy kick. Another kindred dish you might encounter in humble restaurants is "jeyuk bokkeum", closely resembling pork bulgogi. While jeyuk bokkeum is considered a simple and satisfying meal by Koreans, it has surprisingly garnered enthusiastic praise from some foreigners, with claims of it being the best Korean food they've ever tasted.

It's worth noting that while there are several Korean dishes with the prefix "bul," most of them are known for their fiery spiciness, except for bulgogi. While bulgogi refers to grilling over fire, in other dishes, "bul" signifies a level of spiciness that can burn your mouth. Those are indeed quite fiery, and many Koreans opt to avoid them. So, if you encounter a menu item starting with "bul" and order that assuming it's similar to bul-gogi, be prepared for potential fire in your mouth. In extreme cases, you might even need to call the fire department (Korea's emergency number is 119). It's human nature to be tempted when told something is off-limits, so if you choose to try it, ensure your travel insurance covers any potential medical expenses.

Galbi, translating to ribs, is a term that carries a delightful duality, representing both a body part and a scrumptious culinary treasure. Strictly speaking, it refers to the bone itself, but in the culinary realm, it signifies the meat adjacent to the ribs, often served with the bone intact. In many instances, the meat isn't pre-cooked but is instead grilled directly on a tabletop grill, reminiscent of the practices observed in pork belly establishments.

When the term galbi is used without any specific mention, it often refers to beef ribs, while ribs from other animals like pork, lamb, or chicken are distinguished by prefixing the animal's name. Within Korean cuisine, there are two main types of galbi: saeng galbi (fresh ribs) and yangnyeom galbi (marinated ribs). The superior quality meat of saeng galbi is typically grilled without any marinade, making it slightly pricier and exquisite choice at most restaurants. However, internationally, Korean galbi is commonly known as marinated ribs, and both beef and pork ribs are beloved grilled dishes among Koreans.

While galbi may be slightly chewier compared to tenderloin or sirloin cuts, it employs a particular cutting and sheathing method that enhances its texture, resulting in a truly satisfying eating experience. Furthermore, marinated ribs, whether crafted from beef or pork, tend to be more tender owing to the marinating process, effectively tenderizing the meat.

In Korea, beef galbi, alongside tenderloin and sirloin cuts, can command hefty prices, particularly at upscale restaurants. Cheaper establishments may opt for American or Australian beef, while more luxurious venues favor the premium quality of Korean beef. A single serving, though not always sufficient for one person, can range from $40 to $70 and even surpass $100 at extravagant establishments. Despite the considerable cost, the undeniable melt-in-your-mouth goodness of galbi makes it an unparalleled delicacy.

Due to its expense, high-end grilled beef is often meticulously prepared by the staff, a departure from the casual ambience of samgyeopsal restaurants. Grilling yangnyeom galbi presents its own set of challenges, as the seasoning can easily burn. Even in the hands of professionals, certain parts may char, necessitating impressive scissor skills to remove only the inedible portions and minimize waste. As previously mentioned in the pork belly story, the enjoyment of galbi extends beyond the meat itself. It is commonly accompanied by a variety of vegetables, side dishes, and often complemented with cold noodles or stew.

Bibimbap is an enticing dish that showcases a harmonious arrangement of various ingredients atop a bed of rice, resulting in a flavorful ensemble when mixed together. While vegetables, known as "namul," form the basic foundation of bibimbap, it can also feature meats, eggs, and an array of other additions tailored to individual preferences. A dash of gochujang or soy sauce is commonly added, although it can be adjusted or omitted according to personal taste. Almost always present is the touch of sesame oil, contributing to the characteristic of bibimbap. Similar to a sandwich, there is no fixed recipe for bibimbap, allowing for endless possibilities for customization and personalization.

In a way, bibimbap can be considered a kind of fast food. While it may require individual cooking of each ingredient, many of these components fall under the category of "ban-chan", which are dishes prepared in larger quantities and stored in the refrigerator for multiple meals. This makes bibimbap a convenient choice for individuals living alone or in situations where time or energy for cooking a main dish is limited. By combining an assortment of side dishes from the fridge, adding sesame oil and gochujang, and mixing it with rice, a satisfying bibimbap can be created. Adding a fried egg on top further enhances the overall experience. As for rice, Korean households often have frozen rice stored in the freezer or convenient vacuum-sealed packages of instant rice available. Simply heating it up in the microwave provides the rice component for bibimbap. So, if bibimbap happens to be on the menu for a family meal at home, it could be because the person responsible for cooking, such as your mom, may not be feeling well that day.

Of course, bibimbap can also be enjoyed as a luxurious main dish when made with high-quality ingredients. Its beauty is undeniable, with carefully selected and artfully arranged ingredients that render it one of the most visually appealing Korean dishes. However, once served, there's no avoiding the inevitable act of mixing it all together, potentially disrupting its pristine presentation. So, before indulging, don't forget to quickly snap a photo with your smartphone to capture its beauty, and then bravely embrace the delightful chaos of blending all the flavors together.

If bibimbap represents the homemade fast food, then "gimbap" takes the crown as the true Korean fast food available in restaurants. Gim, also known as laver, holds a significant place among the various seaweeds that Koreans consume in abundance, including miyeok (sea mustard) and dashima (kelp). Gim refers to both the seaweed that grows in the sea and the dried and thinly stretched seaweed sheets resembling paper. To meet the high demand, gim is extensively cultivated through aquaculture on the southern coast of the Korean Peninsula, where sprawling farms of laver, sea mustard, and kelp can even be seen on satellite images. Among the three countries engaged in laver farming—South Korea, China, and Japan—South Korean laver stands out for its exceptional quality, resulting in annual exports worth approximately $700 million. While Koreans commonly use gim as an ingredient in gimbap or enjoy it as a side dish after grilling with oil and a sprinkle of salt, many foreigners also relish it as an enjoyable snack on its own.

Seaweed is recognized for its substantial environmental benefits, such as absorbing carbon dioxide from the atmosphere and helping to mitigate seawater acidity. South Koreans, with their high levels of plastic and energy consumption, may find solace in their consumption of seaweed, viewing it as a way to offset their environmental impact. (Interestingly, South Korea's extremely low fertility rate, while posing challenges for the country, can be considered a positive factor for the planet in terms of population control and resource sustainability.)

Gimbap, a culinary marvel, is crafted by layering a thin sheet of seaweed with rice, adding a variety of ingredients, rolling it into a cylindrical shape, and then slicing it into bite-sized pieces. While typically featuring around five or six ingredients, the variations are practically limitless. Much like the versatile sandwich, gimbap opens up a world of possibilities, with Korean restaurants offering dozens of creative types. It combines the flavors of rice and side dishes into a convenient and portable package. Gimbap can be enjoyed without chopsticks and easily eaten by hand, making it a practical choice for on-the-go consumption, whether in the car, on the train, or even while working at the office.

While purchasing gimbap is incredibly convenient, crafting it at home can be quite time-consuming, earning it the label of a 'slow food.' Consequently, Koreans often reserve the preparation of gimbap for special occasions, such as school picnics for their children or when the entire family embarks on a long journey. The cost of gimbap can range from as little as $3 to $4 per roll. Due to its shareable nature, it is often advisable to order a variety of gimbap when dining at a restaurant, allowing your group to sample different flavors and ingredients.

Gimbap and the Japanese dish maki or norimaki have similarities, but they also have distinct differences. Maki usually contains one, two, or three ingredients along with rice, whereas gimbap incorporates a wider variety of ingredients. In terms of size, gimbap is generally larger than maki. Maki commonly includes different types of fish like tuna and salmon, whereas gimbap generally does not include fish as a filling. However, there are variations of gimbap, such as tuna gimbap, which uses cooked and canned tuna, while maki typically uses raw tuna.

The origins of gimbap and maki/norimaki are subjects of debate. One viewpoint suggests that both Korea and Japan have a long history of consuming seaweed, leading to the independent development of similar dishes. Another perspective proposes that Korean gimbap was influenced by Japan's maki after its introduction to Korea. Additionally, there is a theory that Korean gimbap was introduced to Japan in ancient times. Despite the debate surrounding their origins, gimbap and norimaki have diverged into individual dishes with their own characteristics. (It is evident that California rolls, in particular, represent an Americanized adaptation of norimaki.)

Visiting South Korea can pose challenges for vegetarians, and adhering to a strict vegan diet can be even more difficult. Vegetarian options are often limited in restaurants, with meat commonly used as an ingredient, even if it's not immediately apparent, such as in broths. However, there are some viable choices for vegetarians, notably gimbap and bibimbap. Gimbap offers several meatless varieties (though eggs are usually included), and there are also meatless options available for bibimbap. By tactfully requesting "gogi ppejuseyo" (without meat please) when ordering bibimbap, vegetarians can effectively communicate their dietary preferences.

Street food in South Korea offers a plethora of options, and

one of the hottest choices is "tteokbokki," consisting of simmered rice cakes. "Tteok" refers to steamed or boiled grain flour
that is molded and enjoyed as a snack, dessert, or an ingredient
in main dishes. Among the various types of tteok, "garae-tteok"
stands out as a simple, long, white, cylinder-shaped rice cake.
Tteokbokki is commonly made by stir-frying garae-tteok with
gochujang (red pepper paste) and sugar, resulting in a flavorful
and spicy dish. However, the spice level is usually moderate and
not overwhelming for foreigners, unless specifically seeking out a
restaurant known for its spiciness. Accompanying the rice cakes,
you'll often find "eomuk" (fishcake), vegetables, and boiled eggs.
Sometimes, ramyun noodles are also included, but without the
soup.

Indeed, "sundae" (or soondae) is a unique Korean dish that
might be misleading for those expecting ice cream. Sundae refers
to Korean sausage made by filling pig's intestines with a mixture
of vegetables, "dangmyeon" (glass noodles), and pig's blood. It is
a ubiquitous street food item and can be prepared in different
ways. The most common method is steaming the sausage, which
is then enjoyed plain. However, sundae can also be stir-fried or
used as an ingredient in soups.

"Hotteok" is a beloved Korean snack. It is a pancake that is filled with melted sugar and crushed nuts, creating an irresistible combination of flavors and textures. Koreans savor hotteok for its warmth and comforting taste on chilly days. Similarly, "bungeo-ppang", also known as carp bread, is a popular winter treat. Despite its name, it does not contain fish. Instead, bungeo-ppang is baked in a fish-shaped mold, giving it its recognizable appearance. The filling consists primarily of red beans that are mashed with sugar, resulting in a sweet and satisfying treat.

If you're sweating like a pig in Korea during the summer, you gotta treat yourself to some "pat-bingsoo" (red bean bingsoo). This icy dessert is crafted with meticulously shaved water or milk, and crowned with boiled red beans soaked in sugar. Bingsu literally means "ice water", and although there are other bingsu flavors that use fruits, teas, or coffees instead of red beans, red bean bingsu stands out as the most preferred choice. While red beans may not be a common pantry staple in most countries, the Koreans are onto something with the versatile ingredient. True, plain red beans on ice might sound unexciting, but the red beans in pat-bingsu are slow-simmered with tons of sugar, granting it a satisfyingly sweet flavor.

Hold on to your taste buds, because we're about to dive into the world of "hodugwaja," the Korean walnut pastry. This intriguing treat is like a cookie or bread, but with a twist. Crafted using a special mold shaped like a walnut, it cradles a heavenly combination of flour dough, walnuts, and red beans. Once exclusively found at highway rest stops, these goodies have now spread across the country, ready to satisfy your cravings. Trust me, nothing surpasses the taste of a freshly baked walnut bun that's still warm and gooey. Just a word of caution, though: take small bites because these treats can be piping hot and leave you with a burn to remember. Korean snacks like hodugwaja, bungeo-ppang, and hotteok are true originals, hailing from a land that didn't have a strong Western bread culture.

One of the culinary highlights you must not miss in Korea is "hoe", which refers to raw food. While you can enjoy raw beef, the most common choice is "saengseon-hoe", raw fish. Earlier, I mentioned the distinction between Korean and Japanese soy sauce. Both countries have well-developed soy sauce cultures, offering various types based on production methods and aging. However, the key difference lies in the ingredients. Korean soy sauce is made exclusively from soybeans, while Japanese soy sauce incorporates wheat or barley along with soybeans. Another notable contrast is the use of "meju" in Korean soy sauce, whereas Japanese soy sauce employs a specific mold instead of meju. In Korea, leftover soy sauce is used to make doenjang, while in Japan, it is simply discarded. Korean soy sauce can be made at home without machinery, but Japanese soy sauce requires specialized factories and a compression process, resulting in fewer leftovers. Interestingly, Japan also has its own doenjang called "miso," which is made separately from soybeans and includes ingredients like rice, barley, and flour.

Just as the distinction between soy sauce and doenjang/miso in Korea and Japan reveals culinary variations, the preparation and consumption of raw fish also showcase notable differences. The key disparity lies in the aging process of raw fish. Korean hoe is relished "immediately" after the fish is caught and filleted, while Japanese sashimi is allowed to age for a day or two before being savored. This contrast contributes to the varying textures and flavors. Korean hoe tends to be chewier, while Japanese sashimi offers a softer, more indulgent taste. In terms of serving, Japanese sashimi is typically enjoyed with minimal accompaniments such as soy sauce and wasabi, whereas Korean hoe is often dipped in various sauces like chogochujang and ssamjang, accompanied by vegetables like perilla leaves and lettuce. It's worth noting that Korean hoe is commonly paired with soju, while Japanese sashimi finds its perfect match in sake.

While we've explored a variety of beloved Korean noodle dishes, one notable omission is "jjajangmyeon", a staple found in Korean Chinese restaurants. Jjajangmyeon features a delectable combination of shredded pork, onions, and assorted vegetables stir-fried with "chunjang", a savory black bean sauce similar to China's Tianmian sauce. This tantalizing mixture is then tossed with boiled noodles to create a truly satisfying dish. Although commonly associated with Chinese cuisine, jjajangmyeon holds a special place in the hearts of Koreans as one of their favorite comfort foods. While it may not surpass the popularity of kimchi-jjigae, doenjang-jjigae, or ramyun, it certainly ranks among the top 10. Notably, Chinese restaurants are well-known for pioneering food delivery, and jjajangmyeon has become a representative moving day food. In the past, when people faced greater financial hardships, it was a frequent meal for the working class when dining out. To add a cinematic twist, in the movie "Oldboy," had the protagonist subsisted on jjajangmyeon for 15 years instead of fried dumplings, the tension may have been slightly alleviated. (Of course, considering the circumstances, "dumplings" were a more fitting choice.)

Legend has it that 'jjajangmyeon' originated from a Chinese restaurant nestled in Incheon's Chinatown back in 1905. While it may bear Chinese influences, 'jjajangmyeon' is heralded as a distinctively Korean creation rather than an authentic Chinese dish. Actually, there isn't an exact counterpart to 'jjajangmyeon' in China, although there are variations that share some similarities.

Jjajangmyeon is not an isolated example. Many Chinese restaurants in Korea have adeptly adapted their dishes to cater to Korean preferences rather than strictly serving authentic Chinese cuisine. While there are indeed some Chinese restaurants that excel at preparing genuine Chinese food, the majority of the over 20,000 Chinese restaurants in Korea specialize in Korean-style Chinese cuisine. If you have an appreciation for Chinese cuisine and are intrigued to taste the black noodles often featured in Korean movies and dramas, it's worth visiting a Korean-style Chinese restaurant at least once. Why leave when there's still so much more to explore in Korea? Stay one more day and let's see what other adventures await you.

# 15.

# Seoul: The City That Never Sleeps

As I mentioned before, in South Korea, you can casually leave your laptop or phone on the cafe table and it magically stays put. (Some people call it 'K-moral', others call it 'K-CCTV'.) Whether it's the power of conscience or the watchful eye of CCTV, South Korea takes security to a whole new level, 24/7.

Life is short, and time flies, especially for travelers. If your style of travel is to cram in as many experiences as possible with as little sleep as possible, Seoul is the perfect destination for you. Seoul is a city where the lights never go out.

To kick things off, Seoul offers an abundance of restaurants and shops that keep their doors wide open throughout the night.

(Convenience stores, understandably, are the real night owls, open 24/7 with only rare exceptions.) Even if not operating around the clock, you'll find numerous eateries and bars that stay open until midnight or even until the early hours of the morning. Unless you're staying in an ultra-exclusive neighborhood, you'll always find a restaurant within a leisurely stroll, especially in Seoul, that satisfies your late-night cravings. So, let go of any thoughts about dieting for a moment, in Korea, please indulge in four meals a day!

It's quite amusing to discover that certain restaurants proudly display a sign that boldly claims "open 24 hours," yet they don't quite live up to that promise. It appears that for some owners, having the label "open 24 hours" serves as a symbol of prestige or success for their establishment. Undeniably, the phrase itself carries a sense of assurance, as it suggests that a restaurant staying open for such extended hours must be prosperous and thriving. However, it can be a source of amusement to find the small print beneath the grand proclamation stating something along the lines of "Break time 02:00 - 07:00." (Are they doing it on purpose to be funny?)

In Seoul, you can find a few markets that remain open round

the clock, although their operating hours have been slightly adjusted during the pandemic. One notable example is Namdaemun Market, the oldest and largest traditional market in the city, boasting a rich history spanning over 600 years. With its vast array of more than 10,000 small shops, the market caters to both locals and tourists alike. Additionally, a multitude of eateries are available, catering to the needs of vendors, shoppers, and visitors. Namdaemun (Gate), also known as Sungnyemun, holds great significance as the primary entrance to the city center during the Joseon Dynasty and proudly bears the title of Korea's National Treasure No. 1. At Namdaemun Market, you can find virtually anything your heart desires. As a retail hub during the day and a wholesale center at night, it sees bustling activity around the clock, although not all shops operate 24/7. However, it's worth noting that while the market offers a diverse range of goods, you might find Dongdaemun Market to be a more suitable destination for satisfying your shopping cravings.

Dongdaemun Market is a sprawling and monumental destination. It first emerged in 1905 as Korea's inaugural modern market, and its sheer scale can perplex even the locals when it comes to pinpointing its exact boundaries. Comprising several interconnected markets, each with its respective name, Dongdaemun Market has become an intricate tapestry of commerce. Notable market sections such as Pyeonghwa Market, Gwangjang Market, Bangsan Market, and Jungbu Market are clustered around Dongdaemun Station, accessible via Lines 1 and 4, as well as Dongdaemun History and Culture Park Station, which is served by Lines 2, 4, and 5. A stone's throw away from the bustling markets lies the iconic Dongdaemun Design Plaza (DDP), an architectural marvel envisioned by the celebrated British architect Zaha Hadid.

Dongdaemun Market, a haven for fashion enthusiasts, is renowned for its extensive range of clothing offerings, where you can discover an astonishing array of styles and sizes at incredibly affordable prices. Whatever you're seeking, be it any style imaginable, you'll find it within the market's sprawling expanse. If you find yourself overwhelmed by the sheer size of this bustling marketplace, make your way to Dutamall or Miliore, two popular destinations that offer a more focused shopping experience. Prior to the pandemic, these establishments pleased shoppers by staying open until the early hours of the morning, but their operating hours had since been adjusted to close around midnight or 2 am. But, currently, almost every market has resumed their full late-night operations once again, while some sections still close their doors regularly.

Seoul offers a diverse range of parks and hills that are equally captivating during the late hours. The city is blessed with parks located on both the southern and northern banks of the Han River, which flows through the heart of downtown Seoul. This abundance of green spaces provides plentiful opportunities for nighttime adventures. On pleasant evenings, you can head to one of the riverside parks, unwind with a refreshing beer, and immerse yourself in the enchanting night views of Seoul. (Remember, I mentioned earlier that public drinking is legal in Korea.) Within these parks, you'll find 24-hour convenience stores that offer a selection of alcoholic beverages and light snacks, including cup noodles.

Among the notable sections of the Han River Citizen Park are the vibrant districts of Yeouido, Ichon, and Banpo. Yeouido and Ichon offer splendid views of the iconic Wonhyo Bridge, which gained fame as a filming location in Bong Joon-ho's film, The Host. In Yeouido, you can also embark on a nighttime boat ride, where the allure is heightened under the cover of darkness, and enjoy a charming dinner while cruising the river. The Ichon district presents breathtaking vistas across the river, while the Banpo district captivates with the Banpo Bridge adorned with its enchanting fountains and floating islands (Sebitseom).

But, a truly enchanting spot for a nocturnal wander is Naksan Park, nestled along a section of Seoul's historic castle wall. Perched atop a gentle hill, Naksan Park provides a pleasant ascent that doesn't require arduous climbing. You can easily reach the park with a mere 10-minute stroll from Hyehwa Station on Subway Line 4, or you can embark on a scenic 30-minute walk along the city walls from Dongdaemun Market. From this vantage point, gazing upon the modern skyscrapers that adorn downtown Seoul while standing within the remnants of a centuries-old castle is a remarkable juxtaposition of the city's past and present. Naksan Park proves to be a splendid destination both during the day and at night, where its allure is heightened. However, the park's enchanting beauty truly shines under the starry sky, making it an Instagrammable hotspot for capturing stunning moments of Seoul's past and present in perfect harmony.

Seoul is brimming with vibrant neighborhoods that are

buzzing hangouts for young people, offering a wide range of options for late-night dining, cozy cafes, and trendy bars. In addition to well-known areas like Insadong and Itaewon, there are also emerging districts to explore, such as Gyeongridan-gil, Hannam-dong, Seongsu-dong, Sangsu-dong, Iksun-dong, the hidden alleys near Sinyongsan Station, and the charming neighborhoods of Bukchon and Seochon, located on either side of the majestic Gyeongbokgung Palace. Choose a couple of these lively enclaves that are conveniently located near your accommodation and embark on an exploration of their unique offerings. While the labyrinthine streets may occasionally confuse you, there's no need to worry. Your trusty smartphone will guide your way, and even if you happen to wander off track for a while, you can be confident that stumbling upon a metro station is only a matter of time (unless luck plays an unexpected trick).

Naturally, Friday and Saturday nights take center stage with their vibrant energy, but Seoul never fails to provide a lively atmosphere, even on other days of the week. People can be found drinking, dining, and enjoying themselves well past midnight. You might wonder, "Do Koreans ever sleep?" Well, it is true that Koreans tend to get less sleep. According to statistics, the average

Korean gets around 7 hours of sleep, which is notably shorter than in other countries. This sleep deprivation is particularly prevalent among teenagers who carry heavy study loads. On average, Koreans sleep approximately 30 minutes less per day compared to their counterparts in other countries. (Perhaps that's the reason behind my constant fatigue?)

Aside from that, there's one more question that may arise while wandering the streets of Seoul at night: What are all those red crosses? You'll notice an abundance of them, as red crosses adorn multiple locations. While Koreans are accustomed to their presence and don't find it peculiar, it can be quite perplexing for a foreigner encountering them for the first time. Do they imply the existence of a cemetery in every neighborhood? Or perhaps every Korean is a member of the Red Cross? These thoughts might cross your mind.

No need to worry, those are actually churches. While Catholic churches may not have them, it's quite common for Protestant churches in Korea to proudly display neon red crosses atop their buildings, as large and high as possible. While churches in other countries don't do this, why do churches in Korea?

Christianity in South Korea has a relatively short history, with

Catholicism arriving in the late 18th century and Protestantism in the late 19th century. The introduction of Protestantism was largely influenced by American missionaries, and the denominations that brought it to Korea often prioritized faith over extravagant church buildings. While mega-size churches with an enormous number of believers emerged later in South Korea, the earliest churches found their humble beginnings in general-purpose buildings or shared spaces within existing structures. Even today, you can find a lot of small churches occupying a floor or two of commercial buildings across the country. As a result, there were limited symbols or visual cues to indicate the presence of a church.

It wasn't until the 1960s that the trend of adorning plain church buildings with neon crosses began to gain prevalence. The exact reason behind the choice of red as the predominant color remains speculative, with one theory suggesting that it was selected for its affordability among the various neon color options. Nevertheless, as the Protestant population in South Korea experienced substantial growth, accompanied by a significant increase in the number of churches, a sense of competition emerged, prompting the adoption of larger and more prominent symbols. Presently, South Korea is home to an estimated 10 million Protestants and 4 million Catholics. (Around 8 million follow Buddhism, while over half of the country's population does not have a religious affiliation.)

Over the past decade, the increase in the number, size, and brightness of red crosses on churches has ignited controversy, particularly in relation to light pollution concerns. It's not uncommon to spot more than 10 red crosses in a single glance in some areas. While regulations have been implemented to control nighttime lighting and advertising, church crosses have received an exemption, possibly due to political considerations, including the influence of Protestant votes. (South Korea boasts an estimated 50,000 churches, surpassing the number of Starbucks or McDonald's locations but falling short of chikin restaurants.) As a result, the South Korean night sky is illuminated by the brilliance of tens of thousands of red crosses. Rest assured, these crosses symbolize churches, not cemeteries, so there's no cause for alarm.

Another exciting destination to experience at night is a hypermarket. No matter where you find yourself in the world, exploring local markets is always a delight, and in Korea, hypermarkets offer an equally captivating experience compared to traditional markets. The three major chains - E-Mart, Lotte Mart, and Homeplus - are worth a visit. These hypermarkets surpass the scale of supermarkets found in other countries and display a vast array of products. The atmosphere within is distinctively different from that of Carrefour or Walmart. (Carrefour and Walmart made unsuccessful attempts to enter the Korean market and eventually withdrew. Their failures have been extensively discussed in numerous business books as "localization failures." Costco stands as the sole foreign retail giant to survive in Korea.)

Korean hypermarkets offer a wide array of products, ranging from manufactured goods to fresh produce such as fruits, vegetables, meat, and fish. Additionally, they provide clothing, toys, bedding, appliances, and a plethora of other items. It is challenging to identify specific products that Korean hypermarkets do not sell, as their offerings are comprehensive. (There are specialized retailers that focus on curating and selling unique items not generally found in hypermarkets, and I will discuss these stores later.) The assortment of ingredients for various Korean dishes, as well as the extensive selection of ready-made meals for convenient home heating, is truly impressive.

These hypermarkets operate every day, except for a few days

mandated by the government to protect traditional markets. They usually close around 11 p.m., so it's worth stopping by for a quick browse. And chances are, you won't leave empty-handed. Ideal items for foreigners to buy at Korean hypermarkets include ramyun noodles, laver (plain for making gimbap, lightly toasted for snacking), coffee on a stick (a sweetened Korean-style coffee made with instant coffee, sugar, and cream), and Hbaf almonds (with the H silent, and Honey Butter Almonds being the top-selling flavor among various options). You can also try a pear drink, known as 'crushed pear,' which, although not a major seller in Korea, is surprisingly exported. Foreigners often refer to it as the IdH drink due to the resemblance of the Korean word for 'pear (bae)' in a running style to the English letters IdH. This drink is especially in demand among those seeking hangover relief. Initially developed and sold by a Korean beverage company, Coca-Cola now holds the rights and has recently launched an even more potent hangover-relieving version called "I.d.H.," gaining big popularity. With over 400 hypermarkets scattered throughout the country, a little searching will make it easy to find one nearby.

If you're interested in grooming or beauty products, there's a place you should visit before heading to the hypermarkets - Olive Young. With 1,200 stores nationwide, Olive Young is a Korean drugstore specializing in health and beauty products. They have everything that is cheap enough to be sold in a department store and small enough to be bought in bulk at a hypermarket. You'll find cosmetics from various brands, both domestic and foreign, as well as a plethora of accessories related to health, beauty, and grooming. Olive Young also caters to men with a decent selection of products. Unlike France's Sephora, which focuses primarily on cosmetics, Olive Young has a relatively smaller collection of cosmetics, but abundant health and hygiene products. It can be compared to Japan's Matsumoto Kiyoshi, which originated as a pharmacy and thus stocks a higher proportion of medicines, although Olive Young has fewer medicinal products. Additionally, you'll find a variety of food items and unique products that might leave you wondering their purpose. Anyway, you can't help but buy something, even if it's just a face mask sheet.

The store is popular among foreigners, and you'll find that some of the staff can speak English, Japanese, and Chinese. At the checkout, they may ask if you have a "membership card," but as a tourist, it's unlikely that you have one. The membership card only offers about a 1% mileage on your purchase, so it's not worth obtaining unless you plan to make frequent visits. Instead, keep an eye out for any special promotions or discounts available. It's worth noting that Olive Young often has extended operating hours, with some stores staying open until 10 or 11 pm, allowing for convenient shopping even in the evenings.

When it comes to shopping in South Korea, there are a few things to keep in mind. While the country, especially Seoul, has a high cost of living, some items are exceptionally expensive, while others are surprisingly cheap. For example, the price of fruit in Korea is notoriously high. Compared to sunny European countries, you can expect to pay three to four times as much, and sometimes even ten times as much. Prices for fruit in large supermarkets might surprise you, but they can be double in high-end department stores. To give you an idea, a single strawberry can cost around $2 (note, not per pack), while an apple or pear can cost between $5 and $7, a cantaloupe can go for $20 to $25, and a peach might be $4 to $5. Even imported fruits are not cheap, and blueberries and cherries, for example, can cost several times more than in the US or Europe. Bananas are one of the few affordable fruits in Korea. However, it's worth noting that Korean fruits are incredibly sweet and delicious, which is why many Koreans find fruit tasteless when they travel abroad.

On the other hand, oysters are a prime example of an incredibly affordable item in Korea. In Europe and the United States, oysters can cost between $4 and $5 per piece in restaurants, with some varieties being even more expensive. Even at markets, oysters are commonly sold by the dozen. However, in Korea, oysters are sold by weight rather than by number. In supermarkets, a bag of 20 shucked oysters costs around $5. While Korean oyster may be smaller, they're still less than a tenth of the price of oysters in other countries where they are more expensive. At seafood restaurants in Korea, a plate of oysters (note, not a single one) usually costs around $15, and at more upscale restaurants, a couple of oysters per person are often provided for free as a side dish.

Why are oysters so cheap in South Korea? Well, turns out they're farmed in huge quantities in many parts of the coast, especially in the south. And although Koreans love them raw, the slightly less-than-fresh ones get thrown into a batter of flour and egg and baked or fried. Any leftovers? No worries, they're frozen and later thrown into soups and stews. So if you're an oyster lover who's been held back by the steep prices elsewhere, it's time to hit up Korea and chow down on all the shelled goodness you can handle. And speaking of chowing down, while some Koreans may give their oysters a squeeze of lemon, most prefer to dip them in choguchujang (red chili pepper paste with vinegar) for a real kick in the taste buds.

Besides oysters, what else can you buy in Korea that's exceptionally cheap? I've racked my brain, but I'm coming up empty-handed. If there's something in Korea that's exceptionally cheap besides oysters, it's probably not a product, but a service. Like, for instance, getting your hair done at a salon. Trust me, compared to the US or Europe, you're getting a steal here. Guys can get a trim for just $10-20, and ladies can expect to shell out $20-30. And if you're feeling particularly brave, you can even score some color or a perm for just $40-80. Now, there are some uppity salons in Gangnam that'll charge you a small fortune, but they're pretty well-hidden, so don't worry too much. And the cherry on top? Korean salons are not only affordable, but they're also super friendly, super fast, and super stylish. So why not treat yourself to a little pampering?

Finally, I've got some good news and some bad news for you. First, the good news: Taxis in Korea are dirt cheap! So even if you stay out until midnight when the buses and subways stop running, you won't have to worry about breaking the bank on a taxi ride back to your hotel. Now for the bad news: Due to multifaceted reasons, it has become quite a challenge to snag a taxi, particularly between 10 p.m. and 1 a.m. So, you have two options. Either you can pace yourself and stick to moderate fun, opting for the subway instead, or you can go all out and party by 1 or 2 a.m. (Or there's always option three: stay out until 5 a.m. and hop on the first subway).

# 16.

# From Screen to Korea: Must-Watch Movies and Dramas Before Your Trip

It's not uncommon to see someone being released from prison in Korean movies and dramas. It could be a thief, a politician, or an ordinary person, such as a housewife. It could be an office worker who embezzled public funds, a drug dealer, or even a murderer. The length of their sentence can vary from a few months to several decades. Sometimes, they are left without anyone to greet them, but more often than not, someone is there waiting for them. After exchanging greetings, whether it be an affectionate hug, a cordial handshake, or a respectful bow, the person waiting outside the prison usually hands them a white cube in a disposable plate or plastic bag. The recipient takes a big bite of it. It's tofu.

It's unclear when the practice of serving tofu to those returning from prison began, and it's also unclear why, but there are several theories. Some say that the white color of the tofu signifies a clean life ahead, others that the protein-rich tofu is meant to replenish the nutrients they lacked while in prison, and some suggest that the filling and easily digestible nature of tofu is meant to prevent those released from prison from overeating suddenly and causing digestive issues. However, my favorite and most plausible literary interpretation is this one. Tofu is made from soybeans. You can make tofu out of soybeans, but you can't make soybeans out of tofu, which means that the act of feeding them tofu is meant to prevent them from going back to their sinful past lives.

Now, I know what you're thinking. We cannot turn a steak back into a cow, cheese back into milk, wine back into grapes, kimchi back into napa cabbage, etc. So, of all occasions, why tofu? But hold on, there's more to this story. See, soybeans are like the grain version of a ball and chain in Korea - they symbolize imprisonment. The term "eating kongbap (rice with soybeans)" is a figure of speech that means prison in Korean culture. For instance, if you come across the line "Do you want to eat kong-bap?" in a Korean movie, it doesn't mean that the characters are discussing a restaurant menu, but rather that they are warning one another not to engage in activities that could lead to incarceration. Interestingly enough, Korean prisons do serve kongbap (I can't speak from personal experience, but I'm fairly certain that it's a staple dish and is served regularly, if not at every meal). Prisoners also should be provided with a somewhat balanced diet, and soybean is the most affordable and nutritious protein source available. This is why soybeans have come to be associated with imprisonment, and why tofu has become a symbol of life outside of prison, at least in Korea.

Another frequent scene that might appear unusual to Western audiences but is commonplace in Korean movies is the "hoesik," where coworkers gather at a restaurant or bar after work to eat, drink, and chat. In Korean culture, this is a regular occurrence, extending beyond a simple company or team dinner, as it may be translated in English.

In some other countries, it's typical for colleagues to grab a couple of drinks or a slice of pizza, settle the bill, and go their separate ways. However, in Korea, work parties take on a different dynamic. There's a certain level of persuasion (sometimes coercion) involved, alcohol is often consumed in excess (sometimes under duress), and the night doesn't conclude at just one venue. It involves hopping from one restaurant to another, one bar to another, lasting until the midnight or even wee hours of the morning. Moreover, the majority of the expenses are covered by the company, turning it into an "extension of work" rather than a pure social gathering.

Of course, not everyone enjoys this kind of work culture, and excessive drinking can lead to many problems. Nowadays, the landscape is different from what it was in the past. However, if you happen to miss a work dinner, even if it's a last-minute decision made two hours before, it may be perceived as a lack of loyalty to your company or team leader, or even a deficiency in social skills. Additionally, it remains common for individuals who either don't enjoy drinking or aren't proficient at it to be compelled by their bosses to partake.

Unfortunately, there are instances where excessive drinking leads to unpleasant incidents such as sexual harassment, molestation, or injuries resulting from falling down stairs. Surprisingly, such injuries are often covered by workers' compensation because they are considered an extension of work, even though they are not inherently part of the job itself. (One might wonder, if it's an extension of work, why not conduct it during business hours?) Additionally, the person leading the dinner, typically the one with the most seniority who pays with their corporate card, tends to be overly talkative, often sharing didactic stories that are often meaningless to the listeners. They also insist, holding their drink high in the air, that everyone empties their glasses simultaneously, leading people to strategically sit as far away from the leader as possible.

When Korean work parties continue into the late night, a commonly enjoyed venue is the "noraebang" (Korean karaoke). Karaoke, derived from the Japanese words 'kara' (meaning empty) and 'oke' (short for orchestra), is a form of entertainment that has spread around the world and is widely embraced. Karaoke is commonly more of a "bar" than a dedicated space for singing, often referred to as "a bar where you can also sing." It is commonly found in a large hall with a stage where people take turns singing. Since it's a mix of people who don't know each other, it's considered rude to shout or over-perform. When there are no singers, it can simply function as a regular bar.

In contrast to karaoke venues in other countries, noraebang in Korea has a primary focus on singing. While some noraebangs serve alcohol, many of them are solely for renting out space to sing and do not sell alcohol. The rooms are typically designed for a small group of four or five people, although larger rooms for groups of ten or more, as well as smaller rooms for solo singing, are also available. As the venue is usually filled with people who know each other well, it becomes a place to let loose and have fun without the fear of judgment - either because they're already quite drunk or to entertain their team leader and seniors). There, attendees may find themselves loosening their ties, mimicking the dance moves of K-pop stars, or skillfully playing the tambourine. The noraebang scenes often depicted in Korean movies and TV dramas are not exaggerated at all.

Noraebang is a popular activity in Korea enjoyed by people of all ages and backgrounds. It can be experienced sober or not, during the day or night, alone or with family and friends. Even professional singers sometimes join in. After someone finishes singing, the machine-generated score is revealed, and there's no guarantee that a professional singer will get a perfect score, even if singing their own song (it's not very discriminating). Singing and dancing at noraebang serve as a way for Koreans to release stress, and they take pride in their reputation as a people who excel in drinking, singing, and dancing. (It's a phrase from ancient Chinese literature, and it's almost the only thing Koreans like about Chinese descriptions of Korea.)

Korean-style saunas, known as 'jjimjilbang,' are cultural spaces frequently featured in Korean movies but may be unfamiliar to foreigners. To comprehend jjimjilbangs, we first need to delve into Korea's traditional heating method called 'ondol,' a practice spanning thousands of years. In this method, a fire is lit in a specially designed firebox known as 'agungi,' and the heat circulates beneath the living room or room, warming the floor and channeling smoke up the chimney. Despite its seemingly simple appearance, ondol heating systems come in various types, with a significant amount of scientific knowledge and engineering behind their design—something even modern architects often admire. The heat generated by the firebox was also utilized for cooking purposes, maximizing its utility beyond floor heating. (Separate fireboxes exist that are not connected to the floor, allowing for use without heating the room in the summer.) While this method is efficient and does not pollute indoor air, a downside emerges if the floor is cracked or broken, as smoke can rise and potentially cause carbon monoxide poisoning.

Ondol is deeply intertwined with Korea's sedentary culture, placing great value on the warmth of the floor during the cold winter season. Envision yourself on a chilly winter day, seeking comfort in a room without a fireplace but featuring a heated floor. Faced with the choice, would you opt for a bed raised about a meter from the ground or a snug futon on the cozy floor? This cultural preference extends beyond sleeping to dining and leisure activities, where Koreans often gather on the floor with cushions. Furthermore, it's customary to remove shoes before entering a Korean home, as the floor space is commonly utilized for dining and sleeping arrangements, featuring a low table and futon.

Indeed, while the ancestral methods of cooking and heating with fire pits and wood have been replaced by modern technologies, the cultural influence of ondol has persisted in South Korea. Today, the majority of homes in South Korea are equipped with heated floors as the main source of heating.

A jjimjilbang can be envisioned as a spacious ondol room, commonly found in Korean-style spas or saunas. The main area is maintained at a comfortable temperature, creating a space for relaxation, conversation, and enjoying snacks. Alongside the main room, diverse other chambers offer different temperatures, ranging from very hot (around 70 degrees Celsius, 160 degrees Fahrenheit) to very cold (resembling an igloo). These rooms feature walls constructed from diverse materials, including wood, dirt, salt, and stone. To accommodate guests who are likely to perspire, lightweight clothing is provided by the establishment. Gender division is generally absent, except in the shower or bath area. Popular snacks available in jjimjilbangs include "sikhye", a traditional Korean rice drink, and baked eggs.

Jjimjilbangs not only offer a relaxing experience but also serve as affordable accommodation for travelers or office workers who miss their last train, as they operate 24 hours a day. The cost of staying at a jjimjilbang is usually very low, ranging from $5 to $10 during the day with no time limit and a slightly higher rate at night. This provides a convenient and budget-friendly option for overnight stays.

It's interesting to note that when Koreans visit a jjimjilbang, they often fold their towels into hats and wear them on their heads. Although it's unknown who first utilized towels in this way, the trend gained fame after the 2005 Korean drama, My Lovely Sam Soon, a romantic comedy that remains one of the most beloved Korean dramas of all time. Koreans affectionately call the towel hat 'yangmeori' (sheep head), and there are plenty of tutorials on how to make one available by searching 'jjimjil-bang head towel' on YouTube. Even K-pop stars like Blackpink have been spotted having fun in a jjimjilbang with sheep head towels on their heads (with over 25 million views of the video). If you ever find yourself at a jjimjilbang, taking a selfie with a sheep head towel on your head while snacking on sikhye and baked eggs is a must. When in Korea, do as the Koreans do!

For foreigners watching Korean movies and dramas, one of the most challenging concepts to grasp is the idea of a 'hagwon,' which almost all Korean students attend. In Korea, students not only attend regular school but also go to hagwons. After the regular school day concludes, it's common for almost all students to visit a hagwon. Being fortunate might mean attending only one, and it's not unusual for students to participate in two or more hagwons in a single day. By the time they finish two or three hagwons, it's usually around 9-10 pm.

The term 'hagwon' refers to a place of learning, covering

a wide range of subjects, including foreign languages, music, sports, cooking, computing, art, driving, and more. People of all ages, from children to the elderly, attend hagwons. University students also frequently enroll in hagwons, often to enhance their English language test scores (e.g., TOEFL or TOEIC) or to prepare for their future careers. Many hagwons use terms like 'academy,' 'school,' or 'institute' in their English translations, creating a landscape that might make the whole country seem like a research cluster to a foreigner, as hagwons can be found on nearly every street corner. However, most of them are not actual academic institutions, and the genuine academic institutes in Korea are often not visible to tourists.

Among hagwons, cram schools play a pivotal role in Korea, particularly for teenagers preparing for university entrance exams. In Korea, where education holds high value, having a solid educational background is crucial. Students and parents often feel that regular school classes alone are insufficient to compete with others, compelling them to choose hagwons (because everyone else is doing it). In Korean movies or dramas, if you see a group of students in a place that doesn't resemble a school, like an ordinary commercial building, it's most likely a hagwon.

There's a prevailing belief that hagwon teachers are superior to school teachers as they can focus on content crucial for entrance exams and have the flexibility to adjust the difficulty level of their classes. In contrast, schools follow a set curriculum that must consider the varying levels of all students. Consequently, top-tier cram school teachers often earn considerably more than their counterparts in schools.

With a substantial number of people attending hagwons, the market for private education in South Korea is immense, with an estimated $20 billion being spent on hagwons each year (equivalent to about 30% of the Ministry of Education's budget). On average, South Korean elementary, middle, and high school students spend around $300 per month on private education, creating a significant financial burden for parents and posing mental and emotional challenges for students. The pressure to excel in exams and attend multiple hagwons can lead to conflicts between parents and their children, contributing to high rates of suicide and depression among Korean youth.

Now that you've learned more about Korea, you might find watching Korean movies and dramas even more enjoyable than before. To assist you in preparing for your trip to Korea, I've curated a list of 10 movies and TV dramas worth considering. It was challenging to narrow it down to just 10, and of course, the selection is subjective. You may have already seen some of them, but I encourage you to watch the ones you haven't seen yet and revisit the ones you have. Upon rewatching, you might notice new things. As the saying goes, sometimes all you need to do is cross the one-inch barrier to discover something new and wonderful.

- "Parasite", a film by Bong Joon-ho that took the world by storm in 2019, needs no interpreter—it's a masterpiece. The famous "jjapaguri" dish, made by mixing two different types of ramyun noodles, gained popularity thanks to the film. Its success even led to a cup noodle version of jjapaguri being sold in convenience stores. While it may not quite match the homemade version, if you're feeling curious, why not give it a shot?

- "Squid Game", the 2021 Netflix drama directed by Hwang Dong-hyuk, is a nail-biting thrill ride that will keep you on the edge of your seat for all nine episodes. In episode 3, the game 'ppopgi' (also known as 'dalgona') is a beloved pastime among Korean children—you might even spot some kids playing it around elementary schools if you keep your eyes peeled. In episode 6, you'll come across the term 'kkanbu' (or 'gganbu'), which translates to 'same side'—also the name of a well-known chain of chicken restaurants in Korea.

• "Oldboy", the 2003 film directed by Park Chan-wook, features iconic scenes that have become well-known among Korean movie lovers. While sannakji, a dish made with live small octopus, is a common food in Korea, it's crucial to remember that it shouldn't be consumed like it was in the movie. The dumplings that the main character ate for 15 years are also a common dish found in many Chinese restaurants in Korea. If you're planning on trying jjajangmyeon, a Korean-Chinese noodle dish, you might also want to indulge in some 'gunmandu' (fried dumplings).

• "Memories of Murder", a 2003 film directed by the talented Bong Joon-ho, unfolds a gripping narrative based on a true story that took place in Korea during the 1980s. It follows the journey of a detective on the trail of a notorious serial killer, with Bong Joon-ho's trademark humor sprinkled throughout. In a twist of fate, the killer wasn't actually caught until 2019.

• "1987: When the Day Comes", is a 2017 blockbuster directed by Jang Joon-hwan that narrates the noteworthy story of South Korea's democratization struggle in 1987, a pivotal year in the country's modern history. This gripping film is primarily based on true events and has deeply resonated with Korean audiences. Even if you're not familiar with Korean history, this movie is a must-watch for anyone who appreciates a well-crafted, engaging story.

• "Extreme Job" is a 2019 film that tells the story of a police narcotics unit that goes undercover by opening a chicken restaurant. Directed by Lee Byung-heon (who coincidentally shares the same name as actor Lee Byung-heon), the film has achieved the remarkable feat of becoming the second most watched Korean movie of all time. Out of South Korea's population of 50 million, a whopping 16.26 million people watched it in theaters. Almost every South Korean has seen it, and it's not hard to see why. This movie is guaranteed to leave you craving Korean-style chicken!

\* "My Mister" is a 2018 Korean drama directed by Kim Won-seok. It spans 16 episodes and features K-pop sensation and actress IU (real name Lee Ji-Eun) and "Parasite" actor Lee Sun-Kyun in the lead roles. This emotionally-charged human drama is widely regarded as a Korean classic, with a deeply moving story about a group of people with struggles who find solace and comfort in their connections with each other. Get ready for a rollercoaster of emotions that will have you shedding tears!

• "My Liberation Notes" is a 2022 TV drama directed by Kim Seok-yoon. It's a 16-episode drama written by Park Hae-young, who also penned the acclaimed series "My Mister". Both viewers and critics have praised it for its unflinching portrayal of the exhaustion and ennui faced by young Koreans in their 20s and 30s. While the story starts slowly, if you stick with it, you will be hooked. The show paints a highly realistic picture of daily life in Korea, from the daily grind of commuting to the trials and tribulations of work and drinking culture including "hoesik".

• "Guardian: The Lonely and Great God" is a 2016-2017 TV drama directed by Lee Eung-bok and written by Kim Eun-sook, a legendary Korean drama writer. The show follows the tale of an immortal goblin who has lived for over 900 years and a high school girl who can see the souls of the dead. It's a fantasy drama that defies reality, but it captivated the hearts of Koreans ready to immerse themselves in the writer's imaginative world.

• "Decision to Leave" is a 2022 movie from the acclaimed director Park Chan-wook, who recently won the Palme d'Or for Best Director at the Cannes Film Festival. Actor Park Hae-il, who was a murder suspect in "Memories of Murder," plays a detective who tracks down the case of unnatural death in this movie. Tang Wei, a prominent Chinese actress, also appears in the movie and adds to its star power. It is considered to be the most "mildly flavored" of the Park Chan-wook movies.

# 17.

# Discover K-pop Spots

When PSY's "Gangnam Style" went viral worldwide in 2012, what were the thoughts among the Korean population? Were they pondering, "Finally, the world recognizes PSY's awesomeness," or "I always knew PSY would achieve great success one day," or "Seems like this catchy tune has universal appeal"? Well, not quite. The typical reaction among Koreans was more along the lines of, "What on earth is this?", "Why is this happening?", "They don't even understand the lyrics!", and "What if people start assuming that all Korean men look like PSY?" and so on.

PSY was already a beloved superstar in South Korea long before the world went crazy for Gangnam Style. He had achieved immense popularity with his debut song and continued to release several hit songs throughout his career spanning over a decade. While he possesses a great voice, it is often overshadowed by his unique vocal style. Similarly, despite being a skilled dancer, his modest physique often takes the spotlight over his dance moves. PSY is not only a talented singer and dancer, but also a prolific songwriter and producer, having crafted a great many songs. In addition to his many talents, he possesses a great sense of humor, which shines through, even in his less-than-fluent English. (His humor is even more captivating in the Korean language.)

Nevertheless, no one could have predicted that his music would become a worldwide sensation, with billions of people dancing to his tunes. (PSY himself probably didn't see that coming either.) When PSY rose to global stardom out of the blue, it left many Koreans genuinely puzzled. (Even PSY himself was probably taken aback by his sudden global stardom.)

There were certainly other Korean singers and actors who had already captured the hearts of foreigners before PSY. Korean movies, dramas, and TV shows were prevalent overseas, and the term "Hallyu" (Korean Wave) had been coined by the mid-1990s. However, nobody had achieved the same level of worldwide success as PSY did. Koreans initially found it hard to believe that PSY had broken through, as the term "Hallyu" had been reserved for people in the Asia who shared similar looks and feelings to Koreans. (How unbelievable it was, they would approach every foreigner they met, asking "Do you know PSY?" just to confirm their doubts.)

As time went by, PSY's "international" fame dwindled (although he remains a major star in Korea), and Gangnam Style was seen as a one-off phenomenon. That is, until BTS came along. BTS's incredible success has once again caused some awkwardness for Koreans, who are aware that, although BTS fans might not admit it, BTS's status in Korea was no higher than PSY's in Korea just before Gangnam Style. However, BTS's wave was much more powerful and sustained than PSY's. In any case, Koreans have been convinced by BTS's global triumph that PSY's success was not a fluke, and that K-pop has universal appeal. Concurrently, Korean movies and dramas have also gained immense popularity, further strengthening the faith in K-content. (And it is with this same faith that I am writing this book.)

If you're a die-hard fan of The Beatles, then Liverpool is a must-visit destination. Similarly, fans of Elvis Presley flock to

Memphis, while ABBA enthusiasts make their pilgrimage to Stockholm, and Mozart lovers head to Salzburg. For Gaudi admirers, Barcelona is a must-see destination, while Munch fans find solace in Oslo, and Shakespeare aficionados flock to Stratford-upon-Avon. (If you love Picasso, you'll be torn between all the places associated with his life and work that you want to explore.) And if you're a K-pop fan, there's no better place to experience the genre than in its birthplace of Korea. To help plan your ultimate K-pop adventure, I've compiled a list of must-visit destinations for any true fan.

Before we dive into the details, I have to confess something: South Korea doesn't have the kind of iconic attractions that can captivate almost any tourist, like the ones found in the cities mentioned above. This is partly because K-pop is a relatively new phenomenon that has yet to generate the same level of global allure as the Beatles, Elvis Presley, or Abba. Unlike Liverpool, Memphis, or Stockholm, there is no BTS Museum, Blackpink's Jenny's House, PSY Art Center, or Twice Village that fans can pilgrimage to.

Despite the lack of iconic K-pop attractions in South Korea, K-pop fans living in the country still have some advantages.

While getting tickets to concerts can be challenging, persistent fans can still manage to attend. And even if you fail to get tickets, there is always the possibility of trying again in the future. If you are dedicated enough to check your favorite singer's schedule in advance and have the stamina to stand in line all night, you may even be able to get into the theater inside the broadcasting station where music programs are produced. Fans of the same singer can also band together and place ads in subway stations and newspapers. Additionally, you can send gifts to your favorite stars or purchase limited edition merchandise. Although some editions may be out of reach, even with money, chances of getting the merch are much higher than those of foreigners.

While there isn't a single K-pop "pilgrimage" spot, there are still plenty of places for foreign fans to visit in Korea. One such place is "Hyuga", a cafe in Seoul's Nonhyeon-dong neighborhood that was converted from the former home of BTS members. The baked goods and drinks may not be anything special, but there are traces of BTS everywhere and plenty of notes left by ARMYs. Just a 15-minute walk away from Hyuga, there is "Yujung Sikdang", a restaurant where BTS used to eat before they became famous. Here, you'll find even more signs of BTS, as well as a variety of Korean dishes including pork belly. If you're an ARMY, don't miss the chance to eat where they ate and drink coffee where they slept.

Another place where ARMYs will be opening their wallets is the Line Friends Store, where BTS members are known to have participated in character development. Run by Naver, Korea's Google, these character shops are located in Hongdae, Gangnam, and Insadong. (The Itaewon location is closed.)

The old swimming pool at Seoul National University has become a frequented spot among BTS fans. The pool, which was previously used by university students and nearby residents, had been neglected for the past 30 years. However, after BTS filmed a music video for "Intro: Hwayangyeonhwa" in 2015, the number of visitors increased. Although the university had initially planned to demolish the pool entirely in 2019, and in fact, three of the pool's four walls are gone. But, thanks to the growing popularity of BTS and the efforts of Professor Hong Seok-kyung, who researches BTS, the university decided to preserve it and is working on a project to turn it into a multicultural space. The as-yet-unnamed site is located near Seoul National University's Institute of Molecular Biology & Genetics.

You'll also have the chance to see where the members of BTS spent their summer vacations and filmed their entertainment programs. There's a TV show called "In The Soop" (Soop is the Korean word for forest) that features BTS members on vacation, and the filming location for the second season has been turned into a tourist attraction. Unfortunately, it's not open to the public, but only to those who purchase a special package deal that includes a stay at the nearby Phoenix Hotels & Resorts and a one and a half hour tour of the filming location. With nightly rates ranging from $220 to $400 for two people, depending on the room, and a two-hour drive from Seoul, it may not be a practical or budget-friendly option for most foreign visitors. Additionally, it's unclear how long this package deal will be available.

An unexpected place where you can experience K-pop culture in Korea is in some subway stations. Several subway stations, including Samsung, Gangnam, Hapjeong, Jamsil, and Hongik Univ. on Line 2, Apgujeong on Line 3, and Cheongdam on Line 7, feature advertisements posted by fans of K-pop stars who have raised money to support them. Subway stations close to the star's agency and those with high foot traffic tend to have the most ads. The cost of posting an ad for a month can range from $2,000 to $5,000. But, with over 2,000 of these ads a year, there are almost always at least 100 of them in many subway stations in Seoul. The ads are usually posted around the K-pop star's birthday or debut anniversary and feature stunning photos and messages of support and love from fans. Many people take pictures in front of them, and Samsung Station on Line 2 has the most ads and is the most expensive. Once you've seen the advertisements in the basement of Samsung Station, head upstairs to check out the "Gangnam Style" sculpture. The sculpture is modeled after PSY's hands as he dances while singing Gangnam Style.

In the heart of Seoul's city center, the main store of Lotte Department Store features Star Avenue, a space decorated with handprints and large photos of several K-pop stars, including BTS. If you touch a handprint and wait a moment, a video of the star will appear. Another must-visit location is K-Star Road, a street lined with about 20 teddy bears modeled after famous K-pop stars, located near the Galleria Department Store in Apgujeong-dong. You don't have to go to these two places on purpose, but it's worth taking a moment if you have a trip to the mall.

"Yongma Land" is an unconventional but noteworthy spot associated with K-pop. Located in the northeast corner of Seoul, it used to be a small amusement park that operated for a decade in the 1980s before shutting down due to operational issues. The park was abandoned for some time, but due to its peculiar atmosphere, it has become an unconventional filming location for dramas, movies, TV shows, and music videos. Recently, it has also been utilized as a "studio" for filming. There is an entrance fee and a few other charges. For example, if you go at night, they'll light up the carousel for an hour for about $10. However, if the park is entirely rented out for a movie, entry might not be possible. The park is relatively remote and inaccessible, about two kilometers away from the nearest subway station, but it has been used for filming by many K-pop stars, including BTS, EXO, TWICE, IU, IZ*ONE, and more. If you're a K-pop enthusiast visiting Seoul for around 10 days, Yongma Land could be a unique and exciting place to explore.

As you can see, there is still a lack of specialized venues for tourists interested in K-content. SM Entertainment's SM Town, which used to operate at COEX, has closed down, and pop-up place "House of BTS" was a massive success in 2019, but unfortunately, it wasn't a permanent space. (It attracted 180,000 people during its 80-day run, so why hasn't it returned?) In the fall of 2022, a special BTS exhibit was held for two months in an exhibition space called "Hybe Insight" in the HYBE building, but again, it wasn't permanent. (Mr. President of Hybe, we urge you to build something large and permanent to help fans fill in the gaps while BTS members are away in the military!)

But, there's still some hope for K-pop fans out there! The Korea Tourism Organization just finished building a cultural complex in the heart of the city called HiKR Ground. Not only can you see K-pop exhibits there, but you can also live out your dream of being the star of your own music video - talk about a great photo op! The best part? No admission fee! And get this, in 2025, there's a new theater in town called Seoul Arena, dedicated solely to K-pop concerts. It's gonna be massive, fitting anywhere from 18,000 to 28,000 folks depending on how they configure the space. But here's the million-dollar question: will it be ready in time for when all the BTS boys are off serving in the military? Only time will tell! Fingers crossed!

If you're a die-hard BTS fan and your sole reason for visiting Korea is to catch a glimpse of the sensational group, then fear not - there are plenty of places to quench your thirst for all things BTS. But, most of these spots are located outside of Seoul. You could make the journey to the east coast and drive over 200 kilometers to reach the Hyangho Beach bus stop. This location is where the music video for "Spring Day," the title track from the 2017 album "You Never Walk Alone", was filmed. It takes about two and a half hours to reach this spot by car, and slightly longer if you take the train, but trust me, the effort will be worth it when you get that 'life photo' that you've been dreaming of. Interestingly, this bus stop was initially constructed for the purpose of filming and was later demolished, but when tourists continued to flock there, Gangneung City decided to rebuild it to look exactly like the one in the music video. (The mayor would have been in big trouble if they didn't!) Another must-visit location is Samcheok Maengbang Beach, which is not far from the Hyangho Beach bus stop and is where BTS shot the jacket for their "Butter" album. While it might be a little trickier for foreigners to reach via public transportation, the Ilyeong station is another spot worth checking out. This disused train station was used to film the "Spring Day" music video, so if you happen to be in Seoul on a snowy winter day, you might just get a chance to snap a same photo of "V" kneeling on the snow-covered tracks.

Korea is filled with countless other locations that hold a special significance for BTS fans. From palaces and museums to beaches, theme parks, restaurants, music video sets, and even the zoo where the members played as children - all are popular stops on "BTS tours" for Korean fans. As an ARMY, you're sure to come across at least one or two places that will excite you. While some of these locations may be challenging to reach, the memories you'll make there will last a lifetime - even if they don't quite live up to your expectations.

Before we conclude our K-pop story, there's another genre of K-pop in Korea that's worth mentioning: trot. This style of music is very different from the K-pop you're familiar with, but it's incredibly popular in Korea. In fact, in 2020, BTS was only ranked second among Korean singers in terms of "YouTube views in Korea". The top spot was claimed by a male trot singer named Lim Young-woong, who is virtually unknown outside of Korea but is a household name in the country. There are many other talented trot singers who enjoy immense popularity in Korea as well.

Although it's really hard to explain in a nutshell, trot, a widely embraced genre of music in Korea, can be traced back to the roots of K-pop in the 1930s. During a time when the record industry was booming and radio was beginning to gain traction, trot became the genre of choice for singers who achieved nationwide fame. These songs were a unique blend of Western music, Japanese pop music, and traditional Korean folk songs. Although trot remained a staple in Korean pop music until the 1960s, it experienced a period of stagnation in the 1970s as other genres like folk, rock, ballads, and hip-hop took over. Despite popular trot singers still existing in the 80s and beyond, the genre became primarily associated with those over 50 years old. However, in 2019, trot made a resurgence in popularity thanks to a television station's audition program for trot singers that became a hit with audiences.

Despite its reputation as "tacky" B-grade music and its appeal to older generations, trot has a devoted fan base that cannot be ignored. Concerts featuring famous trot singers often attract tens of thousands of attendees, and fans show their support by purchasing merchandise and visiting places associated with their favorite stars.

The name "trot" is said to have originated from the foxtrot, a genre of dance music, but the current Korean trot has evolved quite differently from its origins. With a history spanning nearly 100 years, there are now many different styles of trot, ranging from the "authentic" trot to blues, R&B, rock, dance, folk, and more. Trot songs are characterized by straightforward lyrics, simple melodies in four-quarter time, and a distinctive singing style called "kkeokk-ki." (This technique has some similarity with the gruppetto ornament of classical music. A note is figured as if it had been split into two or four subsidiary notes. But, it's very hard to explain in words. Just listen to it and you'll understand.) Compared to other genres of K-pop, trot is easier to sing along to, making it a frequent choice for noraebang, even among younger generations.

If you happen to come across a peculiar song while riding a taxi, dining at a restaurant, taking a break at a highway rest area, or tuning in to the radio or TV in Korea, there's a high chance that it's a trot song. To learn more about this genre, you can search for well-known trot singers such as Lim Young-woong, Jang Yoon-jeong, Sim Soo-bong, Tae Jin-ah, Song Dae-kwan,

Na Huna, and Joo Hyun-mi on YouTube. These are household names in Korea and highly recognized for their contributions to the trot music scene.

Whether Koreans are fans of trot or not, they all agree that the genre is definitely 'Korean'. As such, hearing a foreigner sing a trot song can be quite appealing and amusing. If you were to join Koreans at a noraebang for a business outing or similar occasion and perform a trot song, you would likely receive enthusiastic applause for your unexpected choice.

From global superstars BTS to talented trot singer Lim Young Woong, the range of K-pop is incredibly wide and diverse. (And believe it or not, there are even more incredible musicians that you might not be familiar with yet! I apologize for not being able to include all of them in our discussion.)

# 18.

# Curated Collection of
# Seoul's Hottest Spots

If you've followed along so far, you've already become quite the Korea aficionado. I bet you're itching to pack your bags and head over to experience all that this fascinating country has to offer. But before you do, you might be thinking, "Enough with the generalities, buddy. Give me the details. Where should I go to get the authentic Korean experience? And please, spare me the 'check Lonely Planet' cop-out."

To avoid any accusations of lacking kindness, even though this book isn't your run-of-the-mill "guidebook," I'll go ahead and share a list of Seoul destinations that, in my opinion, any foreigner worth their salt should check out. (I won't repeat the places I've already raved about.) This list includes both well-known spots and hidden gems. Remember, it's entirely subjective, and I can't guarantee it will cater to your preferences. If you asked a hundred Koreans for their recommendations, you'd likely get a hundred different lists. Here, I've compiled a quick list of places I'd suggest to my out-of-town friends and explained why. Hopefully, our tastes in travel align.

First things first, if you're a history-and-heritage-culture buff, a visit to the National Museum of Korea is a must. Considered the OG (original gangster) of national museums, it houses countless 'national treasures' dating back hundreds and thousands of years. Clear explanations in multiple foreign languages enhance your understanding of the extensive permanent exhibitions. Allocate at least three to four hours to cover everything, and if you're lucky enough to catch a special exhibition, be prepared to spend an additional hour or two. For fans of Hangeul, the National Hangeul Museum next door is a must-visit. Despite having a relatively new space and a smaller artifact collection, it offers an excellent opportunity to spend a couple of hours delving into the wonderful alphabet, especially if Chapter 11 of this book has inspired you.

For those with an eye for art, both traditional and contemporary, the Leeum (Samsung Museum of Art) is an absolute must-see. The museum cleverly combines 'Lee' and 'museum' to pay tribute to the art collection of Samsung's founder, the late Lee Byung-chul, and his son, the late Lee Kun-hee. At Leeum, you can marvel at a small but impressive portion of their extensive collection, showcased across three buildings: M1, designed by Swiss architect Mario Botta, features Korean antiquities; M2, designed by French architect Jean Nouvel, showcases contemporary art; and the Samsung Child Education & Culture Center, designed by Dutch architect Rem Koolhaas. Leeum stands as a remarkable architectural masterpiece in its own right. Whether you're an art enthusiast or an architecture buff, the quality of the artwork and the beauty of the buildings at Leeum will undoubtedly leave you in awe.

After the passing of Chairman Lee Kun-hee in 2020, his family made a monumental contribution to the country by donating over 23,000 pieces of art. Initially, many Korean people speculated that the family would sell the collection to settle the colossal $10 billion inheritance tax bill. However, to everyone's surprise, the Samsung family decided to donate the massive art collection to the country instead. The collection, valued at a minimum of $3 billion, is already on display at diverse museums across South Korea. Additionally, the Korean government plans to construct the Lee Kun-hee Museum in 2027 to showcase these significant donations.

If you're interested in Korean historical culture and ancient palaces, two must-visit locations are Changdeokgung and Gyeongbokgung. Changdeokgung Palace stands as one of the most beautiful and enduring residences of the Joseon kings. For a truly captivating experience, it is recommended to visit in the fall when the foliage displays a breathtaking array of colors. Even more enchanting is the opportunity to explore the palace at night during select periods, known as night viewing. However, please note that due to the limited number of tickets available, advance reservations are required. Night viewing is immensely popular, making it challenging to secure a reservation. Nonetheless, there are special options available for foreigners, so it's certainly worth a try.

Gyeongbokgung Palace, the first of the Joseon Dynasty's palaces, was initially constructed but later destroyed during the Japanese invasion in the 16th century. It remained neglected until the 19th century when efforts were made to rebuild it. While the palace has not been fully restored to its original state, it still stands as a remarkable example of a Joseon palace. During select periods, Gyeongbokgung Palace is open for night viewing, and foreigners have relatively easy access to this experience.

When visiting Changdeokgung or Gyeongbokgung, a helpful tip is to rent a traditional Korean costume known as a "hanbok" from a rental shop near the palace. Wearing a hanbok allows you to immerse yourself in the historical atmosphere and capture unforgettable memories through countless photographs. These cherished moments will stay with you for years to come.

The Whanki Museum is a small yet impressive museum dedicated to the works of Kim Whanki, a pioneering figure in Korean abstract art and one of the most prominent Korean painters of the 20th century. While it may be a bit challenging to reach by subway, it is a must-see destination for art enthusiasts. After exploring the museum, I highly recommend taking a stroll around the neighborhood to visit Seokpajeong. Seokpajeong is a breathtaking Korean-style garden that once served as the villa of Heungseon Daewongun, the father and regent of King Gojong.

In the vicinity, you'll find a road where a scene from the movie "Parasite" was filmed. It's the scene where Song Kang-ho and his family hurriedly leave the host family upon their return from camping. If you happen to be British, I suggest visiting Scoff bakery, located just around the corner. It's a well-liked bakery in Korea that claims to be a "British bakery," and it could be interesting for you to see if they offer authentic British bread. Is there another restaurant that claims to be 'British' and performs well in Korea? Maybe there is, but I don't know. (How about in your country?) However, there is an intriguing establishment called the London Bagel Museum that enjoys immense popularity, with people often waiting in line for hours to gain entry. Despite the name, as you know, bagels are not originally British, so the origin of the bakery's name remains uncertain.

If you're curious about learning Korea's modern history, I highly recommend visiting the National Museum of Korean Contemporary History. This museum offers a well-documented look at the country's development from the late 19th century to the present day, covering colonization, war, and poverty. It's conveniently located near the stunning Gyeongbokgung Palace. For those interested in the Korean War and the turbulent recent past, the War Memorial of Korea is another must-visit site. Its exhibits focus on the Korean War in the 1950s.

Another meaningful site related to Korea's time as a Japanese colony is the Seodaemun Prison History Hall. Built in 1908, this prison was notorious for its torture, imprisonment, and execution of independence activists during the Japanese occupation. Even after Korea's liberation, it continued to be used as a prison until 1987, with many pro-democracy activists, including former presidents Kim Dae-jung and Kim Young-sam, incarcerated here. In 1998, it opened as a museum.

If contemporary art piques your concern, then the National Museum of Modern and Contemporary Art (MMCA) is a must-visit venue with four locations throughout Korea. The largest location, Gwacheon, sits just outside the city limits but remains easily accessible via subway line 4. The Seoul branch conveniently stands near Gyeongbokgung Palace. The Seoul Museum of Art (SeMA), situated near Seoul City Hall, offers a diverse array of intriguing temporary exhibitions. It's worth noting that RM, a member of the highly regarded Korean band BTS and an art enthusiast, even made an appearance at the David Hockney exhibit held at SeMA. (RM visited a lot of museums in Korea, so you might not be able to check out all of them.) SeMA also houses several offshoots, including the unique SeMA Bunker, an underground bunker discovered during site investigations for a transit center in 2005. Believed to have been constructed in the 1970s as a secret air defense bunker, its existence remained unknown for decades. It was transformed into an art museum in 2017. The entrance to the SeMA Bunker conveniently sits next to the IFC Mall. Another intriguing museum to explore is the Amore Pacific Museum of Art, run by a cosmetics company, which consistently hosts captivating temporary exhibitions despite having a limited permanent collection.

We've discussed the excitement of visiting big box stores like E-Mart, Lotte Mart, and Homeplus, but let's not overlook department stores as well. Shinsegae Department Store Gangnam in Korea had sales of nearly $2.5 billion in 2022, making it the highest-grossing department store not only in Korea but in the entire world. If you assume all department stores are the same, you're mistaken. On weekends and during sales, there are usually crowds of people, with lines sometimes forming even before the store opens. Finding a parking spot can take 30 minutes or more. Some department stores are so crowded that you'd think they were giving something away for free (although they do occasionally offer gifts to loyal customers called VIPs). It can be surprising to find people purchasing luxury items in such a bustling and vibrant atmosphere that may not immediately give off a customary sense of luxury.

It's even more surprising that some people wait in line overnight or in the early morning to enter ultra-expensive luxury brand stores. While wealthy individuals in other countries shop for high-end brands like Hermès, Louis Vuitton, and Chanel in department stores or flagship stores, enjoying their shopping experience with a sip of Evian or Perrier, why do Koreans engage in this practice? The truth is, those who spend the night in sleeping bags are not necessarily wealthy individuals themselves. They purchase high-end handbags with the intention of reselling them for a profit, without even opening the packaging. It's a lucrative business proposition – imagine buying a $10,000 handbag and selling it for $11,000, earning $1,000 for a night's work. Of course, not everyone is inclined to resell. Some people are willing to stay up all night to acquire something that is highly sought-after and unattainable even with ample financial resources. Now, how do the truly affluent manage to obtain these products? They either travel abroad to make their purchases or secure appointments or invitations to each brand's flagship store, a privilege reserved for those with a significant track record.

The Galleria Department Store in Apgujeong-dong, situated in one of Korea's most affluent neighborhoods, stands out from the typical department store experience. Despite its smaller size and annual sales of less than $1 billion, it boasts the highest sales per unit area in the world, primarily due to its emphasis on high-end products. (East wing is more luxurious among two buildings.) Consequently, the crowds at Galleria are not as overwhelming as those at other department stores. If you're interested in observing the fashion and style of Korea's wealthy elite, this is the perfect destination. Begin your visit by exploring the food section located in the basement level of west wing, where the prices of fruits, fish, beef, and other items reach unimaginable heights.

If you have a penchant for large and sophisticated shopping malls, COEX is a must-visit destination. Its vast size can be overwhelming, so it's recommended to familiarize yourself with the mall's maps, conveniently posted throughout the premises. The exterior of the building showcases impressive giant LED screens with exceptional resolution, adding to its allure. Inside, you'll discover a multitude of shops and restaurants, an enchanting library, a decent-sized aquarium, hotels, department stores, and much more.

Indeed, the IFC Mall and The Hyundai Seoul in Yeouido are both beloved shopping destinations that offer compelling experiences. Situated adjacent to each other, these malls provide a wide range of stores and amenities for visitors to explore. Another must-visit shopping spot is the Lotte World Mall in Jamsil. This iconic mall is home to the impressive Lotte World Tower, which stands as the tallest building in Korea. The Lotte World Mall also houses Lotte World, one of the city's premier theme parks. Additionally, the mall features a sizable aquarium, providing a fascinating aquatic experience.

Among the many markets in Seoul, Noryangjin Fisheries Wholesale Market is a must-visit for foreigners who love seafood. South Korea leads the world in seafood consumption per capita, surpassing countries like Norway, Japan, and even eating twice as much as the United States (which may be one of the reasons for Korea's low obesity rate). Naturally, the market attracts a large number of customers with its vast variety of seafood. While the construction of a new building has somewhat diminished its exotic atmosphere, the market still maintains its unique and captivating character. It caters to both wholesale and retail customers, with wholesale auctions mostly taking place in the middle of the night and early morning, while the rest of the day is focused on retail sales. Interestingly, customers can choose and purchase live fish on the first floor and enjoy it right away on the second floor. After buying the fish on the first floor, they can head to any of the restaurants on the second floor, where the fish is expertly prepared as "hoe" (a Korean style raw fish dish) and served with spicy soup, vegetables, and side dishes. While patrons are required to make an additional payment on the second floor, it remains reasonably priced compared to dining at a standard restaurant.

When it comes to exploring a big city, many people want to experience the panoramic views from the highest observation deck available. In Seoul, you have three solid options to choose from. The first is the Lotte World Tower deck, soaring at an impressive 500 meters above sea level. However, it's located on the city's outskirts and comes with a higher price tag. The second option is Building 63's deck, which has held the title of Korea's tallest building for decades and truly comes alive at night. Finally, there's N Tower, perched atop Namsan Mountain in the heart of the city. While it stands at a height of around 240 meters, when combined with the elevation of the mountain, it offers equally breathtaking views as the Lotte World Tower. You can enjoy stunning vistas from every angle, whether it's day or night. To reach the top of Namsan Mountain, you can take a leisurely walk from various directions or opt for a more scenic ride on the cable car.

If you're not particularly obsessed with heights but still desire a remarkable vista, there's a fourth option. Head up to the 13th floor of the Seosomun Building, an annex of Seoul City Hall, where you'll find a cozy observation deck that won't cost you a penny. Additionally, it conveniently sits next to Deoksugung Palace, allowing you to witness both Seoul's past and present simultaneously. (The Seoul Museum of Art is right next door.)

For those who prefer exploring a city on foot, Seoul offers plenty of exciting places to visit. Start your journey in the famous tourist area of Insadong. From there, you can head east to Iksun-dong or venture north to Bukchon, an old neighborhood with a fascinating history. To the west of Bukchon, you will find Samcheong-dong. Just north of Gyeongbokgung Palace, adjacent to Samcheong-dong, lies the Blue House, which has served as the official residence of the South Korean president for a long time. If you continue west from Gyeongbokgung Palace, you'll come across Seochon, an old neighborhood brimming with charm and character. And if you're up for an even greater adventure, journey further west to Inwangsan Mountain. One must-visit spot on the mountainside is The Forest Choso Chaek-bang, a cozy cafe and bookstore situated in an old post that once served as a guardhouse for Seoul's soldiers. The view from the cafe is absolutely breathtaking!

If you're feeling energetic and the weather is favorable, consider taking a walking tour that starts from Gyeongbokgung Palace. This tour will allow you to explore Seochon, make a stop at the Hwanki Museum, and return to Gyeongbokgung Palace via the filming locations of Parasite and The Forest Choso Bookstore. The total walking time, excluding visits to the museum and cafe, is under two hours.

If you're looking to explore a vibrant neighborhood with a youthful atmosphere, Seoul offers plenty of options. Near Seongsu Station on Line 2, you'll find a variety of excellent cafes, restaurants, shops, and small museums, making it a great destination. Additionally, Hongik University Station on Line 2 and Sangsu Station on Line 6 are bustling with clubs, cafes, and diverse shops, attracting a young crowd. The Itaewon area has long been renowned for its international vibe and vibrant nightlife. You can discover wide-ranging hot spots located to the south and north of Noksapyeong, Itaewon, and Hangangjin stations on Line 6. While it's exciting to wander around without a set plan, keep in mind that the area is quite extensive, and the streets can be winding. It's advisable to have at least two or three destinations in mind to navigate more efficiently. (Our thoughts and condolences go out to those affected by the tragedy that occurred on October 29, 2022, in Itaewon.)

There are quite a few places on the outskirts of Seoul that might be of interest to foreigners. The most prominent one is the DMZ. While it may not be a top choice for locals, many foreigners are curious about it. Foreigners visiting the area are often surprised to find that the DMZ is so close to Seoul. It's only an hour's drive from the center of Seoul. The DMZ extends two kilometers north and south of the Military Demarcation Line. It has been untouched for 70 years since the 1953 armistice, creating a huge natural ecological park 248 kilometers long and 4 kilometers wide. It's difficult to visit on your own, but there are several DMZ tour programs for foreigners.

Here's a fascinating tidbit: the barbed wire often seen on the news and during DMZ tours is not actually the Military Demarcation Line. It represents either the Southern Limit Line, which is two kilometers south, or the Civilian Control Line, which is even further south. Surprisingly, there is no barbed wire on the Military Demarcation Line itself. Instead, there are 1,292 small stakes spaced approximately 200 meters apart.

Everland, South Korea's premier amusement park, is also located near Seoul. Now, if you're from cities like Orlando, Los Angeles, Tokyo, Paris, or Shanghai, you may not find Everland particularly noteworthy. However, for tourists visiting from other parts of the world with more than four or five days in Korea, spending a day at Everland is a fantastic option—especially if you've been a roller coaster fan since childhood.

On scorching summer days, the adjacent water park, Caribbean Bay, offers a refreshing oasis. Don't let the whimsical name fool you—it's actually the "world's largest water park" and definitely worth a visit instead of Everland. (You'll probably have the most crowded water experience of your life.) And one important note: no matter how much you love amusement parks, you should never go to Everland on May 5th. That's Children's Day in Korea, and Everland becomes the most crowded place in the country. It's best to leave the weekend to the Koreans and go on a less crowded weekday instead. You can take the subway to Everland, but it's not a good option. It's much faster and more convenient to take a regular bus or shuttle bus.

To conclude this highly subjective list, I'd like to add a word of caution: a common mistake many travelers make is to get caught up in the guidebooks' lists of popular destinations. Just because it's famous, just because other people like it, doesn't mean you'll like it. Remember, you won't be able to see them all anyway. A good place is not necessarily a great place; a great place is a place you genuinely enjoy. While guidebooks can be helpful, it's essential not to rely solely on them. (In that sense, you're a great traveler for picking up this book and not just reading guidebooks. But don't solely rely on my book either!) Use multiple sources and multiple people's opinions, but only you can plan your own trip that you will enjoy the most. And don't feel like you have to do everything you planned. Life often takes us on unexpected paths, and sometimes the most remarkable experiences come from moments of spontaneous serendipity. It is my sincere hope that at least half of your travel plans will be fulfilled, and that the other half will be filled with unexpected delights.

# 19.

# Curated Collection of Seoul's Yummiest Restaurants

With all the mouthwatering Korean food buzzing in this book, you'll undoubtedly want to indulge in a few culinary pleasures. However, the real challenge lies not only in deciding what to eat but also in choosing the perfect place to savor it. It's only natural to crave the same dish but in a more upscale or renowned setting. While we have these 'international' restaurant lists circulating, such as the esteemed Michelin Guide to Seoul. But, let's be honest, the individuals curating those lists are often foreigners rather than authentic Koreans. (They may include a few local judges, but that's a well-kept secret.) So, where in Seoul can you discover those authentic eateries that truly make Koreans' taste buds dance with joy?

Travelers often have their limits when it comes to indulging in the delectable offerings of Korea. Now, if you're willing to loosen your belt and relish four meals a day (or even five if you're feeling audacious), kudos to you! Forget about dieting. However, let's be realistic here: attempting to devour seventeen meals in a single day is a feat achieved only in dreams (or perhaps nightmares). So, my fellow gastronomical adventurer, it's essential to make strategic choices. It's all about selecting wisely.

I must confess, there are plenty of lackluster restaurants scattered across Korea. You know, the kind that leaves you scratching your head, questioning how they manage to stay in business. (Trust me, they might just shut down sooner or later.) Even if you make impeccable food choices, one wrong turn into a subpar eatery can shatter your dreams of a memorable meal. Fear not, for I present to you my personal top 20 recommendations—an entirely subjective list devoid of any reference to others' opinions. (But if you happen to dine at one of these establishments and walk away disappointed, well, that's on them, not on me, my friends.)

These are my selection criteria, folks. Firstly, I only included places that I've personally ventured into. Having resided in Seoul for quite a while, I've had the pleasure of exploring countless eateries. However, trying every single one of them is an impossible feat. There are a plethora of famous establishments out there, but due to a variety of reasons, I haven't had the chance to grace their premises. Hence, I excluded many well-known restaurants with high reputation simply because I have never been there. To the owners of those excluded eateries, please accept my sincerest apologies.

Secondly, I made sure to exclude restaurants with extremely long wait times or incredibly challenging reservation processes. When I say "extremely long wait," I mean enduring an hour-long wait and still not securing a table. And when I mention "incredibly challenging reservation," I'm referring to the frustration of calling a month in advance only to be met with a resounding "fully booked." Koreans have such a profound love for their cuisine that some establishments, which don't accept reservations and require you to stand in line, witness eager food enthusiasts queuing up hours before they even open their doors. (I know you're curious about their locations, but it's best to resist the temptation. Trust me, sacrificing precious hours of your limited travel time is not worth it.) If you happen to call a restaurant and they offer you a reservation two or three months down the line, it's best to throw in the towel. (Even Koreans themselves often utter a disgruntled "Humph!" and give up.)

Thirdly, I made a deliberate choice to exclude exorbitantly expensive establishments. When I say "exorbitantly expensive," I'm referring to places where you can expect to spend $300 or more per person, excluding alcoholic beverages. The majority of the restaurants on this list fall within the range of $15 to $50 per person. (Of course, there are a few exceptions, but they don't exceed $200.) Furthermore, I've decided to omit restaurants located within luxury hotels. While the food in these establishments may be exceptional, the prices are simply too steep considering the overall value they offer.

Fourthly, I intentionally focused on selecting restaurants that specialize in Korean cuisine. While Seoul offers a diverse array of international dining options, including outstanding Japanese, Chinese, Italian, French, Spanish, and more, I deemed it unnecessary to include them all in this list. However, I did include a few noteworthy "contemporary" restaurants that offer innovative and modern interpretations of Korean cuisine, combining traditional flavors with their unique creative flair.

Fifthly, I chose to exclude dishes that are favored by a relatively niche group of Koreans. These particular foods often have a distinct and robust flavor profile, which may pose a challenge for foreigners who are not accustomed to such tastes. While they hold significance within Korean culinary culture, I wanted to focus on more widely accessible dishes that offer a friendly introduction to Korean cuisine for visitors from various backgrounds.

With these principles firmly in place, I have painstakingly curated a list of twenty restaurants in Seoul (with one exception located just outside of Seoul) that I wholeheartedly recommend to foreign visitors. It's worth noting that, since some restaurants have multiple branches, even nationwide, the practical number exceeds twenty. I must confess, I've kept a few surprises up my sleeve, introducing you to some lesser-known (to foreigners, not to Koreans) culinary pleasures that haven't been mentioned in this book until now. The realm of Korean cuisine is incredibly diverse, and I've conducted thorough research to carefully select a variety of restaurants that I urge you to explore. I encourage you to try at least one restaurant from this list, and if you're feeling particularly adventurous, indulge in two or more. Please note that for those requiring reservations, I've indicated as such, but it's always prudent to double-check for any potential closures or changes in operating hours.

Additionally, I've provided descriptions of the quintessential dishes you should consider ordering at each restaurant, keeping in mind an average appetite of TWO adult men. (What a kind-hearted guy am I!) My suggestion? Embrace the rapture of culinary diversity by ordering a generous assortment of dishes and sharing them among your travel companions. Even if sharing meals isn't your usual practice, let this trip be the catalyst for breaking free from routine and savoring the joy of communal dining.

And here's a little insider tip for you: if you happen to dine at one of the restaurants mentioned in the list below, don't forget to proudly present this book to the staff. Will it earn you any immediate special perks? Well, not exactly. However, let me share a little secret with you. The next time I visit that same restaurant and mention that I'm the author of this very book that many foreigners have been carrying around, who knows? Something wonderful might just come my way.

• Pildong Myeonok: Let's kick off with my personal favorite

eatery. Brace yourself for a rendezvous with one of the most renowned Pyeongyang Naengmyeon joints in town, and trust me, the longing for this place consumed me during my two-year sojourn abroad. The distinctive feature of these noodles is their unexpectedly mild flavor compared to other Pyeongyang Naengmyeon joints. Here's the game plan: order yourself a bowl of Pyeongyang Naengmyeon, complemented by a serving of Bibim Naengmyeon and a plate of delectable dumplings. Now, let me share a little secret not listed on the menu—a must-try specialty known as "banban" (half & half). Brace yourself for a tantalizing combination of "suyuk" (boiled beef slice) and "jeyuk" (boiled pork slice), perfectly harmonized for your pleasure. If you're not feeling too hungry, you can skip the Bibim Naengmyeon. Now, prepare your taste buds for a dip into an enigmatic sauce adorned with tantalizing chunks. The dipping sauce may not win any beauty contests, but trust me when I say it's an explosion of flavor. Take pleasure in dunking both the dumplings and the meat into this magical elixir. Keep in mind, my friends, that peak hours may bring about a wait, but fear not, as the high turnover rate ensures the wait is relatively short compared to the length of the line. This gem has been serving yummy dishes since its inception in 1985.

• Woo Lae Oak: Undoubtedly one of the most famous Pyeongyang Naengmyeon restaurants in Korea. The broth here has a thicker consistency compared to Pildong Myeonok. Translating to "house of revisiting," the restaurant's name holds a special meaning, suggesting that dining here may increase the possibility (and desire) to revisit Korea. Since their Seoul-style bulgogi is also exceptional, I highly recommend ordering two servings of bulgogi and two bowls of Pyeongyang Naengmyeon, or one bowl of Pyeongyang paired with one bowl of Bibim Naengmyeon. It's worth noting their unique payment system: post-payment if you order with meat, but prepayment if you opt for noodles alone. So keep that in mind when placing your order. Be prepared for weekend crowds as this place tends to get quite busy. Woo Lae Oak has been satisfying diners since its establishment in 1946.

• Hanilkwan: This historic restaurant holds an indispensable place in Seoul's culinary landscape since its establishment in 1939. Hanilkwan offers a diverse array of dishes. In my humble opinion, their Yukgaejang (spicy beef soup) surpasses all others in the world, even surpassing my mom's version (don't tell her!). Another highlight is their Bibimbap, which goes by the name "Goldongban" on the menu. It's highly recommended for two people to share a Goldongban and a bowl of Yukgaejang, creating a harmonious dining experience. If you're unable to visit the aforementioned two restaurants, Hanilkwan also serves excellent Pyeongyang Naengmyeon. Vegetarian options are available as well, including Pan-fried Dried Pollack, Mung Bean Jelly with Mixed Vegetables, and Spicy Stir-fried Baby Octopus with Noodles. With five locations in Seoul alone, Hanilkwan is easily accessible for a memorable dining experience.

• Byeokje Galbi: Known as one of the finest establishments for "galbi" in Korea, this restaurant lives up to its reputation. However, it's worth noting that dining here comes with a surprisingly high price tag. Since its inception in 1986, Byeokje Galbi has consistently aimed to offer the best (albeit priciest) galbi experience. The quality of the meat is unparalleled, the grilling staff's expertise is remarkable, and the selection of side dishes is equally exceptional. While they offer various cuts of beef, I highly recommend their signature and most extravagant dish, the Seng Galbi (fair warning: it comes with a price tag of over $100 per person). If you're dining with a group, consider trying the Yangnyum Galbi (marinated galbi) and the yukhoe (seasoned raw beef). Once you've relished the meaty bliss, you can savor a small bowl of Pyeongyang Naengmyeon, which is equally exceptional. With the excellence of their noodles, there's no need to visit any other noodle shops mentioned earlier if you choose to dine here. Byeokje Galbi has four locations in Seoul, with the first one conveniently situated between Sinchon Station on Line 2 and Yonsei University. Additionally, their sister brand, Bongpiyang, is also worth exploring. While offering meat of (almost) equal quality to Byeokje Galbi, Bongpiyang comes at a fraction of the price. My personal favorite dish at Bongpiyang is their pork ribs. With over a dozen branches in Seoul alone, you'll have no trouble finding a Bongpiyang near you.

• Budnamujip: If you've ever had the pleasure of enjoying the delectable sweetness and savoriness of marinated ribs at a Korean restaurant abroad, then Budnamujip is a must-visit. While there are plenty of options available tailored to the tastes of the local patrons, for tourists, I highly recommend indulging in their Seasoned Beef Ribs. Once you've relished in the meaty goodness, make sure to order one serving of doenjang-jjigae and one or two servings of "nurungji" (scorched rice). Nurungji is the delightful crispy rice that forms at the bottom of the rice cooker, and Koreans enjoy it as a snack or as a rice substitute by adding water and boiling it. Budnamujip has been serving satisfied customers since its opening in 1977.

• Hadongkwan: This esteemed establishment specializes in gomtang, a classic beef soup that has remained virtually unchanged since 1939. When visiting, indulging in their delectable beef soup is a must, and if you have to choose between the regular and original, we highly recommend the original. While the regular version features plain meat, the original adds an extra layer of rumen, enhancing the overall flavor.

The broth itself remains consistent across both options. Payment is made at the time of ordering, and once seated, your food will arrive in no later than 3 minutes. It's interesting to note that the average Korean diner typically takes around 10-15 minutes to complete their meal at this restaurant. Once your food arrives, feel free to add an "appropriate" amount of scallions to your dish, conveniently provided on the table. If you're unsure about the quantity, a quick glance at neighboring tables can serve as a helpful reference. Don't forget to savor your meal alongside the well-matching accompaniment of kimchi. Hadongkwan has four locations, with the exception of the COEX Mall branch, which operates from 7 am to 4:30 pm. If there's a branch of Hadongkwan near your accommodation, it's perfect for breakfast the next day after a night of drinking.

• Koryeo Samgyetang: If you have a craving for samgyetang, look no further than this establishment. While there are countless samgyetang restaurants in Seoul, some more famous than this one, Koryeo Samgyetang stands out as the epitome of authenticity. Unlike many establishments that tend to overcomplicate the flavor with excessive ingredients, Koryeo Samgyetang stays true to the classic recipe. Since its inception in 1960, it has remained committed to its roots and continues to operate with only two restaurants in the heart of Seoul. The menu offers several options, but don't feel overwhelmed. Simply order the Samgyetang listed at the top, without any additional labels. Keep in mind that the name may also be spelled as Goryeo or Koryo, among other variations.

• Bongchu Jjimdak: We've delved into the world of chicken quite extensively, discussing places like Kyochon, BBQ, and BHC. However, Korea has another immensely popular chicken dish that stands apart from the realm of fried chicken. Enter Bongchu Jjimdak, a franchise that has garnered significant success with its soy-based braised chicken. Established in 2000, the company operates over 150 branches nationwide, with more than 50 located in Seoul alone. The menu offers two types of chicken: bone-in and boneless, and we recommend opting for the former. You can choose from three spice levels: spicy, normal, and non-spicy, but it's advisable to go for the non-spicy option. Sizing options include large, medium, and small, with the small portion serving 2-3 people, the medium portion serving 3-4 people, and the large portion serving 4-5 people. While there are additional toppings available, they are entirely optional. Once you've relished the flavors of the chicken, consider ordering the "nurungji" to round off your meal. At Bongchu Jjimdak, their version of nurungji is not just scorched rice but an appetizing fried rice made with nurungji.

• Narieui Jip or Nari Sikdang: As I mentioned before, if you could only have one meal in Korea, it should be samgyeopsal. It's important to note that there are countless samgyeopsal restaurants across the country. The number of renowned "matzip" establishments is well over a few hundred, and each venue offers its own satisfying experience. In fact, you can always enjoy a satisfying meal wherever you find a lively crowd of customers. This particular restaurant holds a prominent reputation as one of the most favored establishments specializing in frozen pork belly rather than fresh. Be prepared for potential wait times during peak hours, which can stretch up to an hour. The must-try accompaniment to your pork belly is "cheonggukjang" served with rice. Unlike conventional doenjang that requires a lengthy aging process, cheonggukjang is aged for just two to three days, resulting in a bolder flavor and aroma. The original location in Hannam-dong is known as Narieui Jip, while the branches in Cheongdam-dong and Jamsil go by the name Nari Sikdang. Although the names may differ, the culinary offerings at these branches remain nearly identical. Narieui Jip opened its doors in 1986, standing as a testament to its enduring popularity. For a convenient and dependable pork belly experience in your neighborhood, you can also consider Hanam Doejijip, maintaining over 100 branches nationwide.

• Yeontabal: One food that hasn't been mentioned in this book yet is "gopchang". Gopchang is a broad term for animal intestines, and cow intestines are particularly well-loved in Korea. There are several types of gopchang, depending on the specific part of the animal, with the most prized cuts being "yang" (cow stomach, rumen) and "daechang" (cow tripe). These two cuts are commonly sold together, referred to as "yang-daechang" in Korean. If you've never tried cow intestines before, you might initially hesitate, but trust me when I say that charcoal-grilled yangdaechang is an exquisite delicacy. Every foreigner who hesitated, then took a leap of faith and tried it, ended up giving it a thumbs-up. While there are a lot of restaurants specializing in yangdaechang, Yeontabal stands out as the best. They have five locations in Seoul alone. If you're dining with a companion, I recommend ordering two servings of yang and two servings of daechang, accompanied by some soju. It may seem like a substantial amount, but unlike beef ribs or pork belly, where one person commonly consumes about 1.5 servings, in the case of yang or daechang, two servings per one person is standard. And if you still have room for more after indulging in the meat, you can add a side of "yangbap", a delicious fried rice dish. Yeontabal has been serving customers since 2000, offering an exceptional dining experience.

• Jinju Hoegwan: When it comes to Korean cuisine, there can often be debates about which restaurant serves the best dishes. However, when it comes to kongguksu (soy milk noodle soup), there is no contest. Jinju Hoegwan is widely recognized as the ultimate destination for enjoying this delicacy. It has even gained popularity among notable figures, including the late Samsung Chairman Lee Kun-hee and former President Lee Myung-bak. While soy milk noodle soup is a common dish found in many Korean restaurants, Jinju Hoegwan's version is truly exceptional. Their expertise and unique approach are evident in every bowl they serve. If you have already experienced various Korean dishes and are visiting during the summer, I highly recommend visiting this restaurant, which first opened its doors in 1962. It's worth noting that Jinju Hoegwan's soy milk noodle soup is considered one of the pricier kongguksu in Korea, but it costs only around $10 per bowl. Located in the heart of the city center, amidst numerous office buildings, it tends to get quite crowded during weekday lunch hours.

• Hwangsaengga Kalguksu: Here is my top recommendation among the many renowned kalguksu noodle soup restaurants. While their kalguksu are undeniably delicious, it's the "jeon" that truly steals the show. Jeon refers to a variety of ingredients coated in flour and egg wash, then pan-fried in oil. It can be made with diverse food materials such as meat, fish, and vegetables. The dumplings at this restaurant are also exceptionally tasty. Now, let me guide you on how to place your order. I suggest ordering a bowl of noodles, a plate of mandu (seven large dumplings), and a small plate of modum-jeon, which is a multifarious assortment of pan-fried delicacies. This order will satisfy two people and cost you approximately $40. It's important to note that when ordering kalguksu, you should request "one kalguksu, split into two bowls." When the staff is not fluent in English, expressing this phrase in Korean might be a bit challenging. Try your best to convey the message using hand gestures and finger count. Since many people order in this manner, it's likely to be understood. Hwangsaengga Kalguksu has several branches, but the main branch near Gyeongbokgung Palace is the most acclaimed and crowded. It first opened its doors in 2001.

• Samcheongdong Sujebi: This is the most famous sujebi restaurant in the country, known for its long waiting times. Among the scores of sujebi restaurants, none compare to the length of the queue here. Even on weekdays, expect to wait around 30 minutes during peak hours, and even longer on weekends. Reservations are not accepted, and the restaurant does not use numbered tickets either. Instead, you join the line and enter the restaurant in order. However, the wait time is not excessively long considering the length of the line, as the food is served promptly. If you visit with a companion, I recommend ordering two servings of sujebi and one portion of "gamjajeon" (potato pancake). Regardless of whether you order two or three servings, they are served together in a small jar, allowing you to transfer them into your own bowl at the table. You can enjoy the sujebi with the two types of kimchi provided and add some spicy chili sauce for extra flavor. It's worth noting that eating sujebi can be a bit challenging with just a spoon or chopsticks. I suggest trying to alternate between both utensils or even using them simultaneously for a more enjoyable dining experience.

• Wonjo Ilho Jangchungdong Halmeoni Jip: Don't worry about memorizing such a long name. If you take Exit 3 of Dongguk Univ. Station on Subway Line 3, you'll come across several famous "jokbal" restaurants. While most of them offer similar flavors, each has its own subtle variations. (Koreans recognize the subtle differences, and have their own favorite restaurants. Wonjo Ilho Jangchungdong Halmeoni Jip is my personal favorite.) Now, what exactly is jokbal? It's pig's trotters simmered in water with a variety of sauces, often referred to as the Korean version of Schweinshaxe. (The taste and texture are completely different.) Unlike Schweinshaxe, jokbal is served in bite-sized pieces with kimchi and vegetables (instead of Sauerkraut), accompanied by soju (instead of beer). Jokbal is immensely popular in Korea, and you'll find numerous restaurants serving it. Keep in mind that you don't have to specifically visit Jangchung-dong, as there are plenty of excellent jokbal restaurants near your accommodation as well. In general, these restaurants offer jokbal in three sizes: large, medium, and small. If your party size is two, the smallest size should be sufficient. Some places may offer different types of jokbal, including spicy options. It's advisable to choose the one listed at the top of the menu. Additionally, many jokbal restaurants also serve a dish called "bossam", which consists of boiled pork served with kimchi and assorted vegetables. Jokbal and bossam are often enjoyed as meals or snacks, and alongside fried chicken, they are among Korea's favorite late-night indulgences.

• Halmuni Hyundai Nakji Agu Gamjatang: This restaurant indeed has an unusually long name, and even Koreans struggle to remember it precisely. "Halmuni" translates to "Grandmother," while "Hyundai" shares its name with a well-known car company and an apartment building located nearby. While "nakji" refers to small octopus in Korean, this restaurant specializes in Nakji Bokkeum, a spicy stir-fried small octopus dish, not the octopus featured in the movie Oldboy. If you have a low tolerance for spicy food, I advise against trying it. The dish is relatively expensive because they use high-quality small octopus. In addition to Nakji Bokkeum, they also serve Agujjim (spicy braised monkfish) and gamjatang (pork back-bone stew), all of which pair excellently with soju. This restaurant is not widely listed on search engines, but it is conveniently located within walking distance of Exit 5 of Apgujeong Station on Subway Line 3, right next to Shingu Elementary School.

• Hwa Hae Dang: This restaurant is highly acclaimed for its "ganjang gejang," a dish of marinated crabs in soy sauce.

Ganjang gejang is another culinary astonishment that hasn't been mentioned in this book yet. To prepare it, fresh crabs are immersed in a soy sauce mixture simmered with a variety of spices and then cooled. The crabs are left to marinate in the flavorful sauce for an appropriate duration, allowing the exquisite taste to permeate the crab meat. The dish boasts a naturally salty flavor and pairs exceptionally well with rice. While the flavor, appearance, and eating method may be unfamiliar to foreigners, ganjang gejang is a beloved luxury food among Koreans. In fact, it is often referred to as the "rice thief" because its delectable taste entices diners to devour copious amounts of rice in a twinkling. Hwa Hae Dang has a branch in Yeouido, Seoul, while the main restaurant is located approximately 150 kilometers away, near the beach. Another notable ganjang gejang restaurant is Pro Ganjang Gejang, also known as Prosoycrab, situated in Shinsa-dong.

• Jungsik: Jungsik is a prominent fine dining establishment in Korea, eminent for its innovative approach to Korean ingredients. While it incorporates common elements of Korean cuisine, it presents them in creative dishes that are novel even to local diners. The restaurant has been honored with two stars by the prestigious Michelin Guide and has achieved such success that it has opened a namesake location in New York as well. To secure a reservation at Jungsik, it's recommended to book one month in advance. For the convenience of international visitors, the restaurant's website provides a comprehensive description in English. The dinner experience at Jungsik costs around $200 per person, excluding alcoholic beverages, while lunch prices exceed $100. Additionally, Jungsik offers a dedicated vegetarian menu at the same price point as the regular menus.

• Onjieum: While Jungsik is prominent for its inventive take on Korean cuisine, Onjieum specializes in offering more authentic Korean dishes. The restaurant presents a diverse range of culinary experiences, ranging from dishes once exclusively enjoyed by the royal family to those commonly savored by modern Koreans. The former category seeks to recreate the original flavors and techniques, while the latter focuses on showcasing the best of the ordinary Korean cuisine with premium ingredients and refined presentation. Dining at Onjieum will provide you with a deep appreciation for the rich and well-established food culture of Korea. Situated in close proximity to Gyeongbokgung Palace, reservations are highly recommended to secure a table. The dinner experience at Onjieum costs just under $200, while lunch is priced around $100, excluding alcoholic beverages. Instead of a typical wine pairing, the restaurant offers an enjoyable option of a traditional Korean liquor pairing, further enhancing the authentic dining experience. Onjieum has been awarded one Michelin star.

• Evett: This is the only one on our list that features a non-Korean owner-chef. The cuisine, crafted by Australian Joseph Lidgerwood, doesn't strictly adhere to traditional Korean recipes. Instead, it is celebrated for its innovative interpretations that draw inspiration from Korean ingredients and culinary traditions. Dining here comes with a price tag of approximately $200 for dinner, excluding alcoholic beverages, with lunch offerings surpassing $100. Besides the expected wine pairings, there are options for Korean liquor pairings, and the non-alcoholic pairings are anything but ordinary, featuring chef-crafted drinks that incorporate Korean elements. Opened in 2019 and named after the chef's middle name, Evett has earned one Michelin star, though in my estimation, it merits two.

• Mabangjip: This unique restaurant stands out from the others on this list as it is located outside of Seoul. Situated approximately 1.5 kilometers from Hanam City Hall Station on Subway Line 5, or a 30-minute taxi ride from the southeastern part of Seoul, Mabangjip offers a dining experience that takes you away from the bustling city center. With its origins dating back to around 1920, it holds the distinction of being one of the oldest restaurants in Korea. For an affordable price of less than $15, you can enjoy a satisfying set menu at Mabangjip. The set menu includes a meticulous assortment of over 20 side dishes, rice, and doenjang-jjigae. The majority of the side dishes consist of flavorful and refreshing "namul", a variety of seasoned vegetables. Vegetarians will find this offering to be a satisfying meal on its own, while many guests choose to complement their dining experience by adding beef or pork bulgogi. If you are dining as a pair, you can opt for one type of bulgogi, and for a group of four, both options are available. Notably, the bulgogi here is prepared in a low-moisture style, ensuring a distinct and enjoyable taste. The beef bulgogi is priced at around $15, while the pork bulgogi is priced at around $10.

The restaurant is housed in a traditional "hanok" structure, which may initially feel disorienting as you are guided to one of the many minimalist rooms. These rooms are devoid of furnishings, creating a simple and authentic atmosphere. After settling down on the floor (which may be perceived as slightly inconvenient or clumsy for some) and placing your order, the staff will arrive with a large dining table in a few minutes. The table will be adorned with an impressive array of over twenty different side dishes, each offering an appetizing taste and texture. It is important to note that Mabangjip, with its century-old history, is scheduled to relocate in 2024 due to urban renewal. Therefore, it is highly recommended to seize the opportunity to visit and experience this distinguished restaurant before it moves to its new location.

# 20.

# Beyond Seoul:

# Exploring the Best of

# Korea's Regions

If you're visiting South Korea for the first time and have around five days, you can spend all of your time in Seoul. Seoul is big enough and diverse enough that you'll never run out of places to go, things to do, and things to eat, even if you stay for a week or longer. But hold your horses! If you've got some extra time on your hands or you're a seasoned South Korea traveler who's already soaked up the Seoul vibes, it's high time to venture beyond the city limits. Yup, we're talking about exploring what lies outside the bustling capital. Now, where should you head to uncover the best-kept secrets of this marvelous country?

South Korea may not be the largest country out there, but it sure dwarfs some of those pint-sized places like the Vatican or Monaco. We're talking more than ten times the size of Singapore and nearly ten times bigger than Hong Kong. It's over twice as big as Denmark, the Netherlands, and Switzerland. It even outshines Ireland, the Czech Republic, Austria, and Portugal in terms of landmass. This ain't your average 'blink and you'll miss it' kind of country. But let me tell you, with the jaw-dropping highway system and high-speed rail clocking in at a staggering 300 kilometers per hour, there's absolutely nowhere your wanderlust can't take you if you put your mind to it. The only thing left to decide is where your heart desires to wander off to. The possibilities are limitless, my friend!

The first decision you'll need to make is whether you're up for some adventure behind the wheel. Now, when you're exploring Seoul, trust me, driving is the last thing on your mind. But once you venture beyond the city limits, your entire travel experience will transform based on whether you take the driver's seat or not. Speaking from personal experience, I've embraced the thrill of renting cars in nearly every country I've set foot in. I've even dared to take on the challenge of driving in places with different driving directions. But let's face it, not everyone finds joy in hitting the road, and navigating unfamiliar territories can be both mentally demanding and potentially hazardous, especially when you're used to driving on the other side. (So, my friends from the United Kingdom, Ireland, Australia, New Zealand, Fiji, Thailand, Malaysia, India, Indonesia, Singapore, Hong Kong, South Africa, Kenya, Namibia, or Tanzania, it's best to steer clear of driving in South Korea).

If you happen to opt against driving, fear not, for there are convenient alternatives that will whisk you away to your desired destinations. The cities with KTX, Korea's high-speed rail system, are the go-to spots accessible with ease. For fellow travelers seeking memorable experiences, I highly recommend exploring cities such as Busan, Gyeongju, Andong, Jeonju, and Gangneung. While Busan may take nearly three hours to reach from Seoul, the other cities can be reached in approximately two hours.

Firstly, Busan is the second-largest city in Korea, situated on the vibrant southeastern coast of South Korea. If you reside in an area where glimpses of the ocean are rare and you're an avid ocean lover, and if your heart leans more towards the dynamic atmosphere of bustling cities over the tranquility of the countryside, then Busan is a must-visit destination. The city offers a myriad of accommodations providing breathtaking ocean views, catering to a range of budgets from luxurious to more affordable options. And, of course, let's not overlook the tempting seafood cuisine that awaits you. One local favorite is Dwaeji Gukbap, a mouthwatering Korean-style pork soup, akin to a Korean-style Bak Kut Teh. It's crafted with rice and various seasonings, simmering pork bones to perfection for a rich and flavorful broth.

Busan's unique geography is a sight to behold, as the city is predominantly nestled amidst mountains. The city's development has taken place in the narrow spaces between these mountains, leading to various buildings constructed right up against the mountainsides. In fact, even high-rise apartments can be seen perched on the hillsides, showcasing the impressive utilization of space. This distinctive characteristic stems from the rapid population growth during the Korean War when many evacuees flocked to the city. Ironically, what was once a result of necessity has now become a captivating tourist attraction. A notable spot that exemplifies this captivating landscape is Gamcheon Culture Village. Here, you'll encounter a truly beautiful vista where mountains, sea, and densely packed buildings coexist harmoniously.

In Busan, the world's only United Nations Military Cemetery stands as a poignant tribute. It is the final resting place for numerous soldiers who sacrificed their lives in the Korean War, fighting for peace and freedom. The Korean War marked the only instance when a coalition of nations deployed under the banner of the United Nations. Sixteen nations contributed combat troops, including Australia, Belgium, Canada, Colombia, Ethiopia, France, Greece, Luxembourg, the Netherlands, New Zealand, the Philippines, South Africa, Thailand, Turkmenistan, the United Kingdom, and the United States. Additionally, six nations provided hospital ships and medical personnel: Denmark, Germany, India, Italy, Norway, and Sweden. The people of South Korea hold deep gratitude for the citizens of these 22 nations.

Throughout the Korean War, a devastating toll of 40,896 lives from 17 countries (including Norway among the medical donors) was endured, with approximately 11,000 remains interred at the UN Memorial Park in Busan. While many have been repatriated to their homelands, the sacred grounds hold the eternal rest of 2,319 individuals from 11 nations. The UN Memorial Park in Busan stands as a solemn homage, and each year on November

11th at 11 a.m. local time, people around the world face Busan and observe a poignant moment of silence.

The Jagalchi Fish Market stands as the epitome of seafood markets in Korea, celebrated for its lively ambiance and a wealth of enticing catches. Visitors here enjoy the enjoyable experience of handpicking their favorite live fish and then ascending to one of the many dining establishments upstairs to savor their choice.

In the Haeundae neighborhood, a treasure trove awaits with captivating beaches, luxurious hotels, and a variety of charming restaurants. To kick off your Haeundae adventure, the Haeundae Blue Line Park serves as an excellent starting point. Along the former railroad tracks, you can board a sightseeing train that shuttles you to and from the beach, offering a delightful journey. Additionally, seize the chance to ride the Sky Capsule—a charmingly compact train accommodating 2 to 4 passengers—for an extraordinary coastal perspective. From its lofty vantage point, you'll be treated to awe-inspiring vistas of the picturesque coastline. While you can freely hop on and off both the train and capsule with a single ticket, it's worth noting that weekends tend to draw sizable crowds. Adding to Busan's allure, every October, the city takes center stage as the highly esteemed host of the Busan International Film Festival (BIFF), the largest film festival in Asia.

Haedong Yonggungsa temple is conveniently located just north of Haeundae Beach. While it may not be a stone's throw away, a short car ride of approximately 20 minutes or a distance of around 10 kilometers will get you there. Now, this temple may not be a relic from ancient times or boast any fancy cultural artifacts. As a newbie temple built in the 1970s, it may not win any beauty pageants or have that serene temple vibe. There are rumors of an ancient temple on this spot way back in the 14th century, but the evidence is about as scarce as parking spaces during rush hour. But hey, it's got something going for it - a killer oceanfront location! While most temples in Korea are located in the mountains, this one faces the ocean and has a great view. Even the name is eccentric: "Yonggung" means "the Sea God's Palace," the abode of the god who oversees the sea. In short, it has a reputation as an 'unusual' temple, and, interestingly, many curious foreign tourists are drawn to it. (I'm not saying I recommended it, just pointing out its fame.)

Andong, a city steeped in rich heritage, maintains a distinguished lineage of esteemed families, nurtured countless scholars, and proudly upholds the traditions of Korean culture. Its significance was further elevated when the late Queen Elizabeth ⅱ of England graced its grounds during her 1999 state visit, where a remarkable twist awaited her in the form of an authentic Korean birthday meal.

While in Andong, a visit to the Hahoe Folk Village is an absolute must. This charming enclave is adorned with an abundance of hanoks, traditional Korean houses that exude timeless beauty. Nestled within this idyllic village is the famed Hahoe mask, known as Hahoetal. These intricately crafted masks play an integral role in the region's vibrant cultural performances, adorning the faces of actors who bring the stories to life. With a diverse range of designs available, the most renowned Hahoetal is the one portraying a jovial, wrinkled old man with a wide, beaming smile. Such is its popularity that shops across Korea offer souvenirs and keepsakes inspired by the captivating hahoetal.

Andong has left an indelible mark on the world of spirits with its distinctive Andong soju. Unlike the ubiquitous and inexpensive soju found throughout Korea, Andong soju stands as a premium offering, crafted meticulously from rice. (In this book, we've referred to it as 'premium soju'.) This revered elixir graces the shelves of restaurants and souvenir shops across the city. (It is also available in Seoul and even in airport duty-free shops.)

There are two famous dishes in Andong: Andong Jjimdak (soy-based braised chicken) and Gangodeungeo (salted mackerel). The chain restaurant that sells Andong Jjimdak nationwide is the aforementioned Bongchu Jjimdak, but there are hundreds of independently owned Andong Jjimdak specialty restaurants in Andong. (Dozens of them are clustered in Jjimdak Street, and the flavors are mostly similar.) So if you're planning to go to Andong, there's no reason to visit Bongchu Jjimdak in Seoul. Gangodeungeo is coarsely salted mackerel, and it may be peculiar that the inland city of Andong is famous for its mackerel. The name comes from the fact that long ago, the only way for Andong residents to eat mackerel, which spoils very easily, was to salt it on the beach and then transport it. (You can pronounce it in four syllables: "gan go deung eo," but even if you say it roughly, the people of Andong will understand very well.)

If your travels lead you to the enchanting city of Andong, consider immersing yourself fully by spending at least one night at the esteemed Gurume Resort. Among the myriad traditional accommodations in Korea, Gurume stands as a pinnacle of excellence, offering a valuable opportunity to experience a hanok, a traditional Korean house. A night's stay at Gurume is a worthwhile investment, with prices averaging around $200. Rest assured, this expense is by no means exorbitant when compared to other accommodations throughout Korea. If you choose to stay at this hotel, you may also want to explore the Andong Folk Museum, conveniently located within walking distance.

Gyeongju, often referred to as 'the museum without walls,' is a treasure trove of ancient history. As the former capital of the Silla Dynasty, which reigned for almost a millennium until the mid-10th century, Gyeongju holds a special place in Korean heritage. Buddhist culture thrived in Silla, and two notable landmarks showcase its grandeur. Bulguksa Temple, celebrated as one of Korea's most famous temples, stands as a majestic testament to the Silla Dynasty's rich heritage. Another awe-inspiring site is Seokguram, a stone grotto temple housing a magnificent stone Buddha. Seokguram is considered the pinnacle of science, technology, and art of Silla. However, visitors can access only limited parts of it due to the need for preservation.

Within the city of Gyeongju, you'll discover the sprawling tombs of ancient royalty scattered across the landscape. The prominent Daereungwon, also known as the Tumuli complex, encompasses 23 majestic tombs. Among them, the Cheonma-chong, also referred to as the Heavenly Horse Tomb, allows visitors to venture inside, unraveling the mysteries of the past.

For a glimpse into historic Korean village life, a brief 20-minute drive from downtown Gyeongju takes you to Yangdong Folk Village. Designated as one of the seven traditional villages by the Korean government, this remarkable village harbors over 100 well-preserved houses dating back centuries. Similar to Hahoe Village, Yangdong Village remains a vibrant community. Through platforms like Airbnb, you can even experience the authentic charm of staying in a hanok, a traditional Korean house. Both Hahoe Village in Andong and Yangdong Village in Gyeongju received the prestigious honor of being inscribed on the UNESCO World Heritage List in 2010.

If Gyeongsang Province has Gyeongju and Andong, Jeolla Province presents Jeonju. This cultural hub captivates visitors with its vibrant heritage Korean culture, flourishing art scene, and tantalizing culinary scenes. At the heart of the city is Jeonju Hanok Maeul (Jeonju Hanok Village), a picturesque tourist area showcasing a collection of hanoks. These classic Korean houses offer affordable accommodations, charming restaurants, and artisan craft shops, creating an idyllic setting for an immersive and authentic experience. The bustling streets are adorned with an abundance of street food stalls, tempting passersby with a wide array of mouthwatering treats. To truly embrace the cultural ambiance, don't miss the opportunity to rent a hanbok, ancestral attire that allows you to step back in time. Enhancing the cultural journey is the Traditional Wine Museum, where you can sample a variety of indigenous Korean alcoholic beverages and even try your hand at concocting your own unique blend. Please note that reservations and experiences at the museum are currently available only in Korean. It's worth mentioning that the celebrated Korean group BTS once visited this remarkable destination.

Within close proximity is Gyeonggijeon, a distinguished historical site that houses portraits of Taejo Lee Seong-gye, the esteemed founder of the Joseon Dynasty. Immerse yourself in history by exploring the Royal Portrait Museum within Gyeonggijeon, offering a glimpse into the era when royal portraits played a vital role in capturing the essence of Korea's leaders in the absence of photography. Another notable landmark in Jeonju is the Jeondong Catholic Church, built on the sacred grounds of Korea's first martyrdom in 1791. This solemn place of worship, constructed in 1931, serves as a testament to the nation's religious history.

When it comes to culinary experiences, Jeonju leaves no stone unturned. Whether you choose humble local eateries or upscale establishments, almost any restaurant you step into will elate your taste buds with delicious fare. Jeonju takes pride in its generous servings of side dishes, often surpassing those found in Seoul. Be prepared to be spoiled for choice, as some dining establishments offer an extensive array of options that might leave you pleasantly overwhelmed, all at an affordable price.

Located approximately 200 kilometers east of Seoul on the picturesque east coast, Gangneung is an increasingly popular destination for foreign visitors. This coastal city gained international recognition as one of the hosts of the 2018 PyeongChang Winter Olympics and offers a blend of stunning beaches, delectable coffee, and renowned soft tofu. One fascinating aspect of Gangneung is its connection to South Korea's currency. As we've mentioned before, South Korea is the only country in the world where both mother and son are featured on its currency, and

Gangneung is where both were born. The place is an old house called Ojukheon, which is about 600 years old and one of the oldest remaining houses in Korea. A visit to Gangneung would be incomplete without exploring Hyangho Beach, famous for its iconic bus stop featured in a music video by the BTS, situated approximately 20 kilometers from downtown Gangneung.

If you plan to explore the more remote and less accessible destinations in South Korea, driving becomes an ideal option. Before embarking on your road trip, it's essential to acquaint yourself with the requirements for foreigners driving in the country. To drive in Korea, you will need your International Driving Permit, passport, and driver's license from your home country. Additionally, you must be at least 21 years old and have held your driver's license for at least a year before being eligible to rent a car. Having a credit card under your name is also necessary (similar to requirements in many other countries around the world). While 'basic' insurance is mandatory, it's advisable to opt for coverage with higher limits, considering you'll be driving in an unfamiliar area.

South Korea's highways are tolled, but the fees are not as expensive as those in other developed countries with tolls. (Gasoline is relatively costly.) Payment can be made with cash or credit card, but the convenience of using an electronic payment system called hi-pass is notable. Many rental cars come equipped with a hi-pass terminal, allowing you to settle all toll fees at once upon returning the car. (Make sure to check in advance if the terminal is available.) As a hi-pass user, passing through a tollbooth is simplified by moving into the lane marked with blue guidelines.

The speed limit varies by section, with most roads allowing a maximum of 100 kilometers per hour, while certain highways stretch their limits to 110 kilometers per hour. Now, let's talk about those sneaky speed-catching cameras. They are everywhere, and can be identified by two things. First, there are almost always yellow signs warning you that there are cameras up ahead. (Not that it's desirable, but many drivers tend to put the pedal to the metal in camera-free zones, only to slam on the brakes when they see those signs.) Secondly, believe it or not, there are more non-functioning cameras than functioning ones. Actually, when you see the sign and slow down, a few moments later, you may find no camera in front of you or to the side. (But you can find an 'empty' camera box! And, the actual camera locations love to change their minds.) Since you never know where the real cameras are, drivers have no choice but to slow down every time they see a warning sign. (Anyway, I don't know why I'm telling you this. Hey, can you guess?)

So, it's highly advisable to avoid speeding on Korean highways whenever possible. Moreover, they even measure the time it takes for you to zip through two points just to catch those speedy drivers. Despite all these high-tech gadgets, South Korea has a bit of a reputation when it comes to traffic accidents, with a rate that's only slightly higher than Italy's, the reigning champ of traffic mishaps in Western Europe. It's no secret that both Italy and Korea are known for their passionate and short-tempered individuals. So, my friends, let's prioritize safety and enjoy the journey with a little extra caution!

It's crucial to note that specific sections of highways in Korea are designated as bus lanes, primarily around Seoul. These lanes are exclusively for buses, and regular vehicles are not allowed to travel in them. (Technically, you can only do this if you have at least seven passengers in a vehicle that seats nine or more.) Identifying these bus lanes is easy; look out for the solid blue lines marking them. Therefore, don't be deceived by the seemingly empty lane. Other drivers refrain from entering for a good reason. The operating hours of bus lanes can vary from section to section, and it can be challenging for foreigners to spot the signage. That's why it's essential to stay alert and closely monitor other vehicles while driving.

One of the highlights of driving on the highways in Korea is undoubtedly the rest stops. These Korean highway rest areas are acclaimed for their spaciousness and an impressive range of offerings. Alongside the usual amenities like gas stations, restaurants, and convenience stores, you'll also have the opportunity to indulge in the diverse array of street foods mentioned earlier. Moreover, these rest stops often feature enjoyable culinary delights that are uncommon in city areas. But that's not all! They also showcase a wide selection of car accessories, household goods, clothing, and local specialties, allowing you to shop to your heart's content. You might even stumble upon CDs of 'trot' music, a popular genre in Korea, adding a musical touch to your journey. (Though, there may be no items you need to buy other than street food.) Conveniently spaced about 30 kilometers apart, the rest stops on Korean highways ensure you won't have to wait long for the next one. (The farthest rest stop is usually within 50 kilometers.)

Lastly, as you prepare for a road trip in Korea, it's crucial to keep these important facts in mind. Avoid leaving Seoul on a Saturday afternoon and returning on a Sunday afternoon or evening, as it can add at least an extra hour to your travel time, and sometimes even more. Don't assume that roads will be clear just because it's a different day of the week—highways around major cities are often congested during rush hour. Whenever possible, plan your travel outside of Seoul on weekdays to minimize traffic delays.

Now, let's turn our attention to some destinations that are best explored by car rather than taking the KTX. Our first stop is Museum SAN. The name 'SAN' encapsulates Space, Art, and Nature, while also representing the Korean word for mountain. True to its name, the museum is nestled deep within the mountains. Renowned Japanese architect Tadao Ando has crafted a breathtaking structure, complemented by an extraordinary collection of artwork. Notably, it has drawn visits from popular K-pop stars such as RM(Kim Namjoon) of BTS and served as a backdrop for a lot of dramas, movies, and commercials. With a travel time of less than two hours from Seoul, it's an accessible gem waiting to be explored.

For those seeking a truly enchanting and culturally immersive experience, Awon Museum & Hotel stands out as a fantastic choice. This charming establishment comprises several hanoks, traditional Korean houses, painstakingly relocated from other neighborhoods to create an authentic setting. Immerse yourself in history by spending a night in a wooden building that is over 200 years old, with room rates ranging from $250 to $400, depending on your preferred accommodation. For larger groups, the spacious five-person room is available at around $1,000. If you prefer a daytime visit, you can freely explore the premises without staying overnight. Notably, even BTS chose this location for a photo shoot in 2019. Adjacent to Awon, you'll find Soyang Gotaek, another upscale hanok hotel, along with several more affordable hanok accommodations nearby. (Regrettably, the neighboring small hanok hotels in the area do not provide English-language services on their websites.) The drive from Seoul takes approximately three hours, but if you're visiting downtown Jeonju, it's less than a 30-minute drive away. Exploring both Jeonju and the region by both KTX and car is a great idea.

Sokcho, positioned as the northernmost city on the east coast, historically presented a challenge to reach from Seoul. Formerly inaccessible by train and requiring over five hours by car, the opening of the Seoul-Yangyang Expressway in 2017 significantly improved travel time to just two hours and 20 minutes from Seoul. Sokcho offers a stunning coastline renowned for its beauty and delectable seafood dishes. Nearby Yangyang Beach offers a rare opportunity for surfing in Korea. Don't miss the chance to savor the 'Ojingeo Sundae,' a squid-based sundae, not the classic pig intestines version.

For hiking enthusiasts, a visit to Seoraksan National Park is a must. Often dubbed the 'Yosemite of Korea,' Seoraksan unveils its true magnificence during the autumn season when the foliage paints the landscape with vibrant hues. Art aficionados can make a detour to the Park Soo Keun Museum, adding an extra hour to the journey. Park Soo Keun is revered as one of Korea's beloved 20th-century painters.

Boryeong, a city on the west coast, holds its own charm. Just a two-hour car ride away from Seoul, it offers not only picturesque beaches but also a history as a well-attended summer getaway for South Koreans. However, its international recognition soared in 1998 with the inception of the Boryeong Mud Festival. This annual extravaganza spans two to three weeks, usually towards the end of July, where participants gleefully engage in mud-based activities, covering themselves from head to toe. While the mud is believed to contain beneficial ingredients, don't expect an immediate health boost—it's all about the sheer enjoyment. Remarkably, around 300,000 foreigners flock to Boryeong each year to partake in this festival. If you find yourself in Korea during the summer, this is an event you should definitely consider. And fear not if you prefer not to drive, as there are express buses available for convenient transportation to Boryeong.

And finally, we come to the captivating Jeju Island, a true gem of South Korea. Located a mere 50-minute flight away from Seoul, this beautiful island stretches across 73 kilometers from east to west and 31 kilometers from north to south, making it quite sizable. In fact, it proudly holds the title of being South Korea's largest island, falling just slightly short of the dimensions of Hawaii's Maui. Shaped by volcanic activity, Jeju Island boasts the majestic Hallasan Mountain at its center, surrounded by approximately 370 parasitic cones scattered across its landscape. Due to its southern location, Jeju Island exhibits a uniqueness that permeates every aspect, from its climate and culinary wonders to its rich culture and vibrant ecology. Even for Koreans, the island's dialect remains a fascinating mystery, as it differs from the mainland. (Rest assured, though, as Jeju Islanders also fluently speak standard Korean.) Serving as a classic vacation destination for many, the island enjoys an impressive frequency of nearly 80,000 flights per year shuttling between Seoul's Gimpo Airport and Jeju Airport. In fact, there are over 200 flights daily—surpassing the frequency of some subway lines. With such high demand, securing weekend tickets can be quite challenging, so it's advisable to book well in advance if you plan to visit Jeju. In fact, the Seoul-Jeju route ranks among the busiest air routes globally. At its peak, the annual number of passengers traveling between Seoul and Jeju surpassed a staggering 15 million, although this figure has slightly dipped due to the impact of the pandemic.

Indeed, Jeju Island is a treasure trove of tourist attractions that fascinate visitors from near and far. As an island that hosts nearly 700,000 residents, every corner of Jeju holds its own allure. To begin with Hallasan National Park stands as a crown jewel, and there is a mesmerizing array of waterfalls, caves, and parks of varying sizes. The island also features an abundance of pristine beaches, lush forests, picturesque trails, captivating museums, and splendid dining establishments. Moreover, Jeju Island is home to a myriad of unique sites and experiences that cannot be found elsewhere.

One notable site worth mentioning is the Jeju April 3 Peace Park, which serves as a poignant memorial to the victims of the Jeju April 3 incident, also known as the Jeju uprising. This tragic event holds a significant place in the modern history of South Korea. In the aftermath of Korea's liberation from Japanese colonial rule in 1945, the establishment of separate governments in the North and South in 1948, and the ensuing Korean War from 1950 to 1953, Jeju Island, situated apart from the mainland, became embroiled in a profound tragedy. Lasting for over seven years from 1947 to 1954, the conflict involved a complex interplay of soldiers, police, rebels, and residents, fueled by a range of factors including ideological divisions. The consequences were devastating, resulting in the loss of an estimated 30,000 lives, accounting for more than one-tenth of Jeju's population at that time. The Jeju April 3 Peace Park stands as a somber reminder of this painful chapter in Jeju's history.

Jeju Island is famous for its amazing "haenyeo", also known as sea women. These fearless women dive into the ocean without the use of oxygen tanks to gather a variety of seafood, including abalone, sea urchins, conch, and sea mustard. Some of the fresh seafood you'll enjoy on Jeju is harvested by these skilled haenyeo. While there were over 14,000 haenyeo in Jeju during the 1970s, their numbers have drastically declined, with only around 3,000 active haenyeo today. In recognition of their cultural significance, haenyeo were inscribed as a UNESCO Intangible Cultural Heritage of Humanity in 2016. In certain areas of Jeju, visitors can experience a glimpse of the haenyeo's world, although it is not a fully developed tourist program. For those seeking further knowledge, a visit to the Haenyeo Museum offers fascinating insights into the lives and traditions of the haenyeo.

In addition to its colorful attractions, Jeju Island offers a wonderful environment for walking enthusiasts. The Jeju Olle Trail, a scenic walking trail that stretches along the island's coastline, covers a remarkable distance of over 400 kilometers. Explorers can immerse themselves in the island's natural beauty while traversing this trail. Moreover, Hallasan is adorned with numerous parasitic volcanoes known as "oreum," with a dozen of them displaying exceptional beauty. These oreums, typically ranging from 200 to 300 meters in height, provide relatively accessible hiking opportunities. If you are a very diligent tourist and didn't drink too much the night before, you can get up at dawn to climb Seongsan Ilchulbong. It takes around 30 minutes to hike from the parking lot to the summit, where an awe-inspiring sunrise awaits. Even on moderately cloudy days, the experience remains rewarding. Alternatively, visitors can choose to explore Seongsan Ilchulbong during daylight hours, skipping the sunrise expedition.

For soccer enthusiasts, a visit to the Jeju World Cup Stadium is a must. This magnificent stadium, which hosted matches during the 2002 World Cup, offers breathtaking views of Hallasan Mountain and the ocean. It has received high praise, including being hailed as "the most beautiful stadium in the world" by former FIFA president Sepp Blatter during his visit. (I'm sure he's probably said similar things about other arenas.) If you happen to be in Jeju and a K-League game is taking place at the stadium, you're in for an exciting experience. Immerse yourself in the vibrant atmosphere of the matches while savoring some delicious "chimaek" (a combination of chikin and beer). It is common to find available tickets for matches at the Jeju World Cup Stadium even without purchasing them in advance. Fortunately, admission prices are reasonable, with the most expensive seats priced under $20. For a more enhanced experience, consider purchasing a package ticket that includes two seats with a table, along with chikin and two beers, all for around $50.

Jeju Island offers a superb array of fresh and diverse seafood cuisine due to its coastal location. While you can sample various seafood dishes, one that might surprise foreign visitors is the grilled "tong galchi gui". Galchi, also known as cutlassfish or hairtail, is a very favorite fish of Koreans, and while it used to be a commoner's food, it is now quite expensive. Unlike other regions where the fish is typically cut into smaller pieces, in Jeju, the whole fish is grilled and served at the table. If you're dining with a group of around four people, I recommend trying the grilled whole galchi, a visually stunning and delicious dish commonly found in larger restaurants specializing in Jeju cuisine.

Jeju Island is renowned for its native black pig, known as "heukdwaeji", which offers a distinct and flavorful pork experience compared to regular pork. While slightly pricier, it has become a go-to choice for Koreans, as indicated by the prominent signage in Seoul restaurants that proudly serve Jeju black pork. Among the several recipes, Samgyeopsal (grilled pork belly) and

Ogyeopsal (grilled five-layered pork belly) are the most popular. While you may have already indulged in pork belly in Seoul, a visit to Jeju Island presents a special opportunity. It's almost a tradition for every Korean visitor to enjoy at least one meal of black pork samgyeopsal in Jeju. While some prefer to eat it with salt, in Jeju Island, it is more common to savor it by dipping it in "myeolchi-jeot" (a.k.a. "meljeot", salted anchovies), which is often served alongside the dish without your order. (Did you notice, my friend? Indeed, this book commences with a captivating tale centered around samgyeopsal, and ultimately concludes with another intriguing account featuring samgyeopsal!)

This final chapter is the longest among the twenty chapters, yet it only scratches the surface of the multitude of fascinating places that await you in Korea. Such is the abundance of wonders spread throughout the country. Hopefully, your time in Korea will allow for extensive exploration or you can visit Korea more than twice, enabling you to experience the enchantment of all these remarkable destinations beyond Seoul. May your journey in Korea be filled with unmatched experiences and unforgettable memories, creating a cherished chapter in the story of your life!

The end.

# Presenting K!

**All The Korea**
**You May Not See**

ⓒ **Jaeyoung Park 2024**

초판 1쇄 인쇄 2024년 12월 12일
초판 1쇄 발행 2024년 12월 24일

지은이 박재영
펴낸이 김민정
책임편집 유성원  편집 김동휘 권현승
디자인 퍼머넌트 잉크
저작권 박지영 형소진 최은진 오서영
마케팅 정민호 박치우 한민아 이민경 박진희 황승현
브랜딩 함유지 함근아 박민재 김희숙 이송이 김하연 박다솔 조다현 배진성
제작 강신은 김동욱 이순호
제작처 한영문화사

펴낸곳 (주)난다
출판등록 2016년 8월 25일 제406-2016-000108호
주소 10881 경기도 파주시 회동길 210
전자우편 nandatoogo@gmail.com
페이스북 @nandaisart | 인스타그램 @nandaisart
문의전화 031-955-8865(편집) 031-955-2689(마케팅) 031-955-8855(팩스)

ISBN 979-11-94171-30-0  03910